12-15

D1443479

Changing
Reality

Changing Reality

HUNA PRACTICES TO CREATE THE LIFE YOU WANT

SERGE KAHILI KING

QUEST

BOOKS

Theosophical Publishing House
Wheaton, Illinois * Chennai, India

Quest Books
Theosophical Publishing House
PO Box 270
Wheaton, IL 60187-0270

www.questbooks.net

Cover art: *Eye of Kanaloa*, digital art created 2012 with MandalaMaker 2.0 software. Copyright © KAStrick Designs.
Cover artist Kathryn Strick, www.kastrickdesigns.artistwebsites.com. Kanaloa is the God of the Ocean in Hawaiian mythology. The Eye of Kanaloa symbol is said to be healing, as well as a shamanic stargate.
Cover design by Drew Stevens
Typesetting by Datapage

Library of Congress Cataloging-in-Publication Data

King, Serge.
    Changing reality: Huna practices to create the life you want / Serge Kahili King—1st Quest ed.
        p. cm.
    Originally published: Volcano, Hawaii: Hunaworks, 2010.
    Includes index.
        ISBN 978-0-8356-0911-1
    1. Huna. 2. Shamanism—Hawaii. I. Title.
    BF1623.H85K55 2013
    299'.9242—dc23   2012039106

        5 4 3 2 1 * 13 14 15 16 17

            Printed in the United States of America

Dedication

This book is dedicated to the Alakai of Huna International, who have committed themselves to spreading the Huna philosophy, sharing the Aloha Spirit all over the world, and helped in many ways to develop the ideas and techniques presented here.

Table of Contents

Acknowledgments   ix

Part 1 The Shamanic Worldview   1
    1. The Four Worlds of a Shaman   3
    2. A Short Review of Huna Principles 21

Part 2 Changing Reality in the Objective World   37
    3. Knowledge Can Be Power   39

Part 3 Changing Reality in the Subjective World   55
    4. ESP—You Can't Live without It   57
    5. The Telepathic Connection   65
    6. Telepathic Projection   103
    7. Putting Your Aura to Work   125
    8. The Reality of Telekinesis   151

Part 4 Changing Reality in the Symbolic World   171
    9. Tripping through the Land of Dreams 173
    10. Magical Flight   217
    11. Purple Feathers   251

Part 5 Changing Reality in the Holistic World   275
    12. Unity in Diversity   277
    13. A Time to Grok   295

Index   317
About the Author   333

Acknowledgments

With deep gratitude I thank my wife, Gloria, who patiently made me eat when I needed food, skillfully distracted me when I needed a break, and willingly tried new experiments when I needed a subject. Thanks also to my agent, John White, who kept encouraging me to write this book.

Part 1

The Shamanic Worldview

Life Is an Adventure

Be aware of what you are and what you want to be;
You can turn your life around from A to Z.
Nothing is impossible; belief is all you need;
You don't have to trust to luck, just plant the seed.

(Chorus) Oh, Life is an adventure; life is all a dream;
Everything is flexible and not what it would seem.
Dare to give yourself a chance to do the best you can;
Plan the way to live your life and walk your plan!

When the world is getting dark and you are full of fear,
Remember to turn on the light and make things clear.
When you are unhappy and when you're full of doubt,
Fill yourself with energy and then begin to shout:

(Chorus) Oh, Life is an adventure; life is all a dream;
Everything is flexible and not what it would seem.
Dare to give yourself a chance to do the best you can;
Plan the way to live your life and walk your plan!

There's a little secret that's as old as it can be;
Faith can make a mountain move and love can set you free.
So bless the world each morning, and by it you'll be blessed;
Trust the power deep within and then expect the best!

(Chorus) Oh, Life is an adventure; life is all a dream;
Everything is flexible and not what it would seem.
Dare to give yourself a chance to do the best you can;
Plan the way to live your life and walk your plan!

—Serge Kahili King, 1991

Chapter 1

The Four Worlds
of a Shaman

A s many readers know, I was reared and trained
in a Hawaiian esoteric tradition that we call Huna.
Abundant details of this tradition and my training can
be found in my other books. Suffice it to say here that my
adoptive Hawaiian family, the Kahilis, followed a version of Huna that is strongly linked to shamanic traditions
around the world. The equivalent word for "shaman" in
Hawaiian would be *kupua*. What follows, therefore, will
have shamanic underpinnings. For the sake of making
distinctions, the tradition I write about here can be called
Huna Kupua.

Although I have written extensively on the subject of
Huna in relation to many different areas of life, with this
book I intend to go even further in its understanding and
practice. And, no doubt, even more details about my life
may be revealed.

CHAPTER 1

A BIT OF BACKGROUND

One of the most confusing things to students of Huna is the way "Hunatics" (a convenient word coined by a student) look at the world. It confuses my students now and it certainly confused me as I was growing up in this tradition.

When I was a teenager living on a farm, my father would sometimes talk about the crops and the animals around us just like the neighboring farmers would, and sometimes he would talk "to" the same crops and animals as if they were all intelligent beings who could understand and respond to him. Even though I learned to do what he did, it was a good while before I understood the process. There was a time when I found it difficult to concentrate, with all the conversations of trees, flowers, bugs, rocks, and buildings going on. Then, somehow, I learned to switch in and out of that kind of awareness without knowing how I was doing it.

During seven years in Africa, my shaman mentor M'Bala taught me to merge with the animals of the jungle after going into a deep trance state. I thought that the trance was the means of merging until I realized that he was able to do the same thing in the blink of an eye without going into trance at all. Obviously, trance was just a tool and not the thing that caused the shift in experience.

And my Hawaiian kahuna uncle, Wana Kahili (WK), taught me to go on inner journeys filled with wonder and terror and to see omens in clouds and leaves and furniture. Yet he also taught me to be very aware of my waking state and how not to see omens as well, for there are times when that can be just as important.

My father, M'Bala, and WK spent very little time explaining the phenomena they were teaching me to experience. They felt that experience is the best teacher and that intellectual explanation would get in the way. That was a good method for getting me out of my hard head and into my body, but having to deal with the doubts and fears generated by the nonshamanic culture I also lived in slowed down my learning considerably. In my learning and teaching, I have found that satisfying the intellect often lowers the analytical and emotional barriers to learning, allowing for a much faster assimilation of experience. So I spent years in nonjudgmental analysis of my personal experiences and those of other shamans in order to more fully understand what we were doing when we did what we did, so that it could be shared more easily.

The real starting point was WK's teaching that there are four worlds or worldviews (levels or classes of experience) that everyone moves in and out of spontaneously and usually unconsciously, but that shamans consciously cultivate. These are, in Hawaiian, 'ike papakahi (literally, first-level experience), 'ike papalua (second-level experience), 'ike papakolu (third-level experience), and 'ike papaha (fourth-level experience). WK's rough explanation was that these represent, respectively, the ordinary world, the telepathic world, the dream world, and the world of being. For teaching purposes, I have renamed them the "objective," "subjective," "symbolic," and "holistic" worlds. WK also said that all of these worlds are common to everyone, not just shamans, and the difference is only that shamans use them knowingly with purpose. He added that a lot of confusion in people's lives comes from mixing worlds in their thought and speech.

It was my aim to teach a lot of people in a short time about shamanic experience, so even with that helpful start, I had a great deal of filling in to do. Here is a brief résumé of that search and research.

THE SHAMANIC EXPERIENCE

What are we shamans (or Hunatics) doing when we do what we do? We speak with Nature and with spirits; we change the weather and create events; we heal minds and bodies and channel strange beings; we fly out of our bodies, travel through other dimensions, and see what others cannot see; and we pay our taxes, wash our cars, and buy our groceries. Is there a common thread connecting all these widely varying activities, or are they all just a bunch of separate skills?

There is a powerful clue in the first and fundamental principle of Huna. This principle says that "the world is what you think it is." Another more popular way of stating the same thing is that "we create our own reality." Most people who say this don't really accept it fully, because they think it only means that everything bad that happens to them is their fault; and many who accept it with better understanding limit its meaning to the idea that they are responsible for their feelings and experience and that, if they change their negative thoughts to positive ones, they will begin to attract positive instead of negative experience.

Shamans, however, go much further than that. We take that idea to mean that we not only attract experience by our thinking but we also actually create realities. By our assumptions, attitudes, and expectations, we make things possible or impossible, real or unreal. To put it another way, by shifting mindsets, we can do ordinary and nonordinary things in the same physical dimension that we share with everyone else. I repeat that shamans are not unique in doing this. Any apparent uniqueness comes from how we apply our abilities.

The way to change experience and be able to use non-ordinary abilities within a given reality is to shift from one set of beliefs (or assumptions, attitudes, and expectations) about that reality to another set. It sounds so very simple, and it is. The most difficult part—and it can be extremely difficult for some—is to accept the simplicity, because that means changing one's idea about what reality is. The definition I am going to use is very simple: reality is experience. It doesn't matter whether you believe in a world "out there," in a world of telepathic and energetic connections, in a world made of dreams, or a world of oneness. Reality is experience, and experience is reality. Therefore, we can either do something to modify reality in some way in order to change our experience of it, or we can modify our experience in some way in order to change reality itself. And that's what this book is all about.

A MODEL OF MINDSETS

The model I am about to present has been specifically designed to enable modern, urban shamans to make clear and conscious distinctions between reality levels or mindsets. In a society more familiar with and accepting of shamanism this would not be as necessary. The same sort of shifts would be made, but they could be made more intuitively because there would be fewer contradictory mindsets from other philosophies, both religious and secular.

Let's imagine that a modern anthropologist is on an island in the South Pacific studying the native culture. One day the village shaman comes in from weeding his taro patch and tells the villagers that, while he was working, the goddess Hina came down on a rainbow and warned him that a hurricane was approaching; then she turned into a bird and flew away. The shaman moves easily from weeding to talking to the goddess, and the villagers accept it easily because they expect the shaman to be able to weed his taro and also talk to gods. The anthropologist, however, is likely to be stuck in a mindset that can allow for only drug-induced hallucination, mental aberration, fakery, or dramatization of some ordinary perception. The possibility that the shaman actually communed with a spirit is lost to him, as is the ability to do it himself.

As the different worldviews are discussed below, keep in mind that each world can be entered into just a little bit, like dipping your toe into a pool of water, or it can be entered as fully as diving into an ocean's depths.

'IKE PAPAKAHI: THE OBJECTIVE WORLD

This is what most people in modern society would call ordinary reality. Using a meadow in a forest as our metaphor, your purely sensory experience of it as an external reality—the colors of the plants, soil, and sky; the smell of the flowers; the sound of birds; the feel of the breeze on your skin; the perception of movement of a doe and her fawn—would take place in an objective world framework. It would also seem obvious and unquestionable to you when viewing the meadow from this level that the meadow is so many square feet in size, that there are so many trees of certain kinds, that some of them are broad-leafed hardwoods and others are conifers, that so many animals of different sorts inhabit the area, that somebody owns it, and so on. All of these observations would be true, but only at this level of perception. For this first level, as obvious as it seems, is perceivable in that way only because of one fundamental belief or assumption that serves as the framework for the objective world: *everything is separate*. This is the assumption that allows for making classifications and categories, the laws of classical physics, and the various philosophies of cause and effect.

It is often quite difficult for people brought up with that assumption to see it as just an assumption. It seems so obvious that it must be the only truth. But that is the nature of fundamental assumptions. All experience tends to be consistent with one's assumptions about experience. It's like putting on rose-tinted glasses and forgetting you are wearing them. If you never remember that you can take them off, you will always think that rose is the natural and only color the world can be. Inconsistency comes in when one becomes aware, consciously or subconsciously, of other assumptions. When the glasses slip, you start to remember you put them on, or you have a dream about a green world. Then you may open up to the experience of other levels. Shamans are taught as early as possible that the objective world is only one way of seeing.

The idea that everything is separate is very powerful and very useful. It has encouraged travel, exploration, science, industry, and all the miracles of modern technology, including those that brought about the publishing of this book. However, it has also been used to justify slavery, racism, wars, vivisection, pollution, and overexploitation of the earth's resources. Understand that the assumption itself is neither bad nor good. Human beings must make other assumptions associated with value systems before good and bad enter the picture, and those can operate at any level of reality. Looking at our meadow objectively, for instance, you might see it as good because it provides a food source for various animals. Or you might see it as bad because it is taking up valuable space that might better be used for housing or feeding humans. The point is that the use or misuse of the environment or its inhabitants is based on the idea that things are separate and quantifiable according to personal value systems.

Two secondary assumptions of the objective world are that everything has a beginning and an ending and that every effect has a cause. Things are caused to be born or come into being by some act or another and then they die or cease to be. This is a vital concern of objective-world thinking, and so great controversies rage over the physical causes of illness and exactly at what moment a cell or group of cells becomes a human being. Huge amounts of money are spent to determine the social and environmental causes of crime and to preserve historic buildings, because the end of their existence would be a cultural loss. And people undergo all kinds of emotional and financial burdens to uncover the specific trauma of their childhood that makes them unhappy today and to extend the life of the physical body. All such actions make perfectly good sense when viewed in the light of the assumptions previously mentioned, but viewed from other assumptions they make no sense at all.

Some people make the value judgment that the objective world is bad, and so they seek to escape it or diminish it or deny it. In shamanic thinking, however, the objective world is simply one more place in which to operate, and to operate effectively in any world is the shamanic goal. In his or her essential role as healer, therefore, the shaman may use objective-world assumptions to become proficient in such healing methods as massage, chiropractic, herbs and medicines, surgery and exercise, or nutrition and color therapy, without being limited to the assumptions of those methods. We change reality at First Level by changing what we do, verbally and physically.

'IKE PAPALUA: THE SUBJECTIVE WORLD

Now assume you are at the meadow again. This time you are aware of the interdependence of the natural world, of the mutually supportive roles played by the elements of light and shade, wind and water, soil and stone, trees, birds, flowers, and insects. You feel like you are part of that interdependence, not just an observer. Perhaps you feel emotions of peace, happiness, love, or awe. And you are aware of the season and reminded of seasons past and yet to come. If you are a shaman or are sensitive telepathically, you will probably be able to make a greater internal shift and become aware of the auras, or energy fields, of everything in the scene before you and the interplay of those forces as well. You may be able to converse with the plants, animals, and stones, or with the wind, sun, and waters, sharing their secrets and stories. Depending on your background, experience, and skill, you may even be aware of and be able to communicate with nature spirits or devas and the oversoul, or *aumakua*, of the meadow itself. While standing there, you could suddenly witness a scene from a hundred years ago of Native Americans camping in that place after a successful hunt, smoking their pipes around the fire and giving thanks to the Great Spirit. You might even feel that you are/were one of them.

The above examples of subjective-world experience are possible because of the basic assumption of this level, namely, that *everything is connected*, supported by the secondary assumptions that everything is part of a cycle and in transition and that all events are synchronous, or happening at the same time.

In the framework of this worldview, telepathy and clairvoyance are natural facts, as unquestionable as the action of a lever in the objective world. Mental communication with anything that exists, regardless of distance, is possible because everything is connected. Emotions can be experienced because of empathic connection. Auras can be seen and felt because energy is the connection. Past and future lives can be known because life is cyclic and time is synchronous. Death, at this level, is only a transition, part of a cycle, whereas in the objective world death is a finality. Everything about this level is true, but again, only from the perspective of this level. This is why people primarily oriented in the objective world have such difficulty accepting telepathic phenomena and subjective sciences, such as astrology, as facts; it is why people who are primarily oriented in the subjective world find it so hard to explain their experiences to objectively rooted friends. Neither world makes sense when viewed from the perspective of the other. If you are born and you die and that's that, then past lives are nonsense. If the stars are a zillion miles away and you are here on earth, then any influence is absurd. On the other hand, if everything is interdependently connected, then cutting down every tree in sight to build more cities is suicide, and if you have been a member of a different race in a previous life, to hate that race today is hypocrisy. A shamanic way out of this dilemma is achieved through the seventh principle of Huna: "Effectiveness is the measure of truth." Instead of trying to decide which viewpoint is right, the shaman uses whichever one is effective and appropriate to the healing aim at hand.

Shamanic healing methods at this level make use of telepathic suggestions and creative thoughtforms, acupuncture/acupressure, and energy balancing, transfer, or movement by hand or with the use of tools such as crystals and special energy shapes and patterns.

'IKE PAPAKOLU: THE SYMBOLIC WORLD

Here you are in the meadow once more, only this time you let your imagination soar, and you see the openness of the meadow as representing your own openness to love and life; the trees become representations of your inner strength and highest aspirations; the birds sing promises of joy; and in the sunlight is the touch of God upon your brow. You are filled with the beauty of the place, so moved that, depending on your inclinations, you immediately write a poem or paint a picture to capture the mood. You have now shifted into a mindset that has as its basic assumption that *everything is symbolic*. With a shamanic background, you could go further and look for guiding omens in the patterns of clouds, leaves, or bird flights. Or you could do a ritual that would consecrate the meadow and make it an even better healing place for future visitors. A typical shamanic progression of thought at this level is that if everything is symbolic and dreams are symbols, then this reality is also a dream. And one aspect of shamanic skill is to enter into dreams and change them. Someone may ask, of what is everything symbolic? And whose dream is it? It would be correct, at this level, to say that everything is symbolic of everything else, but especially of the perceiver, and that the dream is everything's dream, but especially that of the dreamer. Another symbolic-world way of saying it is that everything in your personal life experience is a reflection of you, including all the people and things around you. To change experience from this level, you can change the symbols, change your interpretation of the symbols, or change yourself so that the reflection changes.

The secondary assumptions are that everything is part of a pattern and exists in relationship to something else, and that everything means what you decide it means. Many research scientists and theoretical mathematicians are rooted in this level. They seek meaningful patterns and relationships in the apparent structure of the universe and frequently ignore, not only the effect on their search of their own decisions about meaningfulness, but also any objective applications of their research. For the shaman or other symbolically minded person, it becomes useful to notice how beliefs are reflected in the body and in life experiences, and how easily conditions and relationships are changed when patterns of belief are also changed.

Shamanic healing methods at this level include all faith, verbal, and visualization therapies, including hypnosis, neurolinguistics, affirmations, guided imagery, placebos, dreamwork, and the use of amulets and talismans.

'IKE PAPAHA: THE HOLISTIC WORLD

This time you are not standing in the meadow, you *are* the meadow. You can feel the sunlight being turned into usable energy by the chlorophyll in your leaves as your roots soak up nutrients from the soil, and you gladly give up your nectar to the bee who gathers your pollen to share with other flowers. As the bee, you enjoy sucking up the nectar, and you know without thinking that some of the pollen will be shared with other flowers and plenty will still be there to take back to the extensions of yourself in the hive. As the bird, you feel the trembling of your throat as you sing your mating song and tip your feathered tail to keep your balance on the pine branch hanging at the meadow's edge. And as the pine, you know that you are not at the edge of the meadow, but are part of what makes the meadow what it is.

This is a tiny sampling of experience at the holistic level. The basic assumption here is that *everything is one*. In practical terms, oneness is your identity. The deepest experience of it is generally called something like "cosmic consciousness," a woefully inadequate attempt to describe a sense of being one with the universe that is essentially indescribable because words and language simply cannot contain the experience. The more shallow and common experience of it is your sense of knowing that you exist. Descartes used a very third-level symbolic approach to justifying the sense of being when he said, "I think, therefore I am." An objective approach might be "I sense, therefore I am." The subjective phrase might be "I feel, therefore I am." At the fourth, holistic level, however, we can probably do no better than Popeye, who said "I am what I am and that's all that I am."

In the holistic world, there is no sense of distinction between you and whatever it is that you identify as also being yourself. To the extent that you are aware of the identification, you are operating in the holistic realm; and to the extent you are aware of "otherness," you are operating in other realms. You may have noticed that in our progression from world to world the sense of separation, quite distinct and a primary attribute of the objective world, grew less in the subjective world (connection = less separate) and even lesser in the symbolic world (a reflection still implies something else that reflects). A person can also have a holistic awareness of what is considered self while simultaneously having a nonholistic awareness of what is "not self." Thus a member of a certain tribe in West Africa can have a holistic identification with his own tribe (that is, he may have no sense of personal identity apart from being a tribal member) and yet have a completely objective and hostile view of another tribe.

While holistic identity is a natural human experience—some people normally extend their sense of identity to personal belongings, family, town, or country—it requires considerable skill to enter and operate consciously in this world. Actors and actresses, whose profession developed out of an age-old shamanic tradition, are the most well-known practitioners of this skill today. In ancient times, and to a certain extent in modern times, shamans were and are able to take on the identity of animals, nature spirits, and archetypes that pass for gods and goddesses. In that state of identification, they have the qualities and powers of those entities. Just as a good actor who is normally shy can convincingly play a confident hero by really getting into the part, so can a shaman attain the strength of a bear or the wisdom of a god by contemplation and acting the part so well that the part acts him. This comes from the second-ary assumptions of this level, that knowing begets being.

As Ralph Waldo Emerson put it, "Do the thing and you shall have the power."

At this level, the shamanic healing modes are primarily of two sorts: channeling, whereby one takes on the identity of a greater healer or becomes one with a greater healing power and then works on someone in a healing way; and what I call "grokking and guiding," whereby one identifies with or becomes the person to be healed and then heals oneself. Needless to say, the latter takes a fair amount of confidence to do successfully. Otherwise, you get so disturbed by the other's condition that you pop out of the holistic level and cannot operate effectively there, or you forget who you really are and take on the other's symptoms without being able to heal. People who are strongly empathic may have this experience often. Many therapists identify so much with the problems of their patients or clients that they take on all the ills they are trying to help cure. When I train my students in healing at the holistic level, I recommend that they limit any identification process to a maximum of ninety-nine percent, so that the "one percent shaman" can always return to the core identity.

MOVING BETWEEN WORLDS

Shifting mindsets or moving between worlds in full consciousness is a subtle and delicate process. An approximation of what goes on is the experience of looking at this page of written material. It is possible for you to read the words and absorb the information, then to check it for typographical and spelling errors, then to notice the type size and style and paper quality, and finally to become aware of the page as part of a book that you are holding in a particular location at a particular time. The only thing that has changed is your perception, which you voluntarily changed in order to change your experience. In moving between shamanic worlds the process is similar. All you do is change what you are looking for and the assumptions associated with your aim.

The biggest obstacle to this and any other shamanic practice is the interference of critical analysis from other levels. It is quite difficult to practice telepathy if you keep telling yourself that ESP stuff is nonsense. Visualization will do you little good if you keep asking, "Am I just making this up?" And it's very hard to make a decent income if you identify yourself as spiritual and you identify money as nonspiritual. In order to move easily and effectively between worlds, you have to practice dropping the assumptions—and the critical analysis deriving from them—of each world you leave before moving on to the next. With practice, lots of it, this becomes virtually automatic. What helps tremendously is loving yourself without reserve and trusting God within you. But of course that is good advice whether you are a shaman or not.

Chapter 2

A Short Review of Huna Principles

~~~

I n all of my books, in some form or another, I teach what I call "the seven principles of Huna," so much so that some people get bored or irritated because they think, "I've heard all that before." If you feel this way, then skip this chapter. The principles will pop up now and then in further chapters, anyway. However, if you are interested in expanding on what you already know and in stretching your mind a bit, then read on.

The principles are really just observations about life handed down orally for untold generations in some cultures and actually written down in various ways for millennia in others—for these ideas do not belong to any single culture. They can be found scattered throughout the writings of Greek and Roman philosophers, in the Old and New Testaments of the Bible, and in the traditions of Taoism, Buddhism, Sufism, and Hinduism, to name a few. They came to me as a complete set of ideas through the Hawaiian culture. What is unique about the particular family traditions that were passed on to me is that I was taught to treat them as a set of tools for changing reality. With that in mind, here are some ways of looking at these principles.

I first learned the seven principles of Huna as a set of ideas from my Hawaiian uncle, William Wana Kahili, but not in the same form as I teach them now.

The first form he taught them in was as seven specific Hawaiian words: *'Ike, Kala, Makia, Manawa, Aloha, Mana, Pono.* By studying the meanings and the roots of these seven Hawaiian words along with common modifiers, one can develop a set of guidelines for turning the essence of Huna into a practical way of changing reality. The problem for me as a student and as a teacher was that these guidelines were learned at a feeling level, the way traditional Hawaiian teachers taught their knowledge in the past. That is, I knew them and could use them, but because of my Western intellectual training I had a difficult time thinking about them and expressing them in English. The first course I taught in Huna was nine months long, and at the end of it all the students were still asking, "What is Huna, really?"

In order to solve this problem I spent a great deal of time condensing these guidelines into simple words and phrases that would be valid in their meaning, be pathways to deeper understanding, and be easy to remember. I will list them briefly, because they will be referred to throughout the book. They do not describe everything about Huna, but everything about Huna can be derived, implied, deduced, or induced from them. If you already know them by heart, please bear with me.

My keywords: Awareness, Freedom, Focus, Presence, Love, Power, Harmony (I have used variations on the last one, but this is my favorite).

My condensed phrases: The world is what you think it is; There are no limits; Energy flows where attention goes; Now is the moment of power; To love is to be happy with; All power comes from within; Effectiveness is the measure of truth.

While this system has made it much easier to teach Huna to people trained in modern educational systems, much of the original flavor is lost, so I will present some other ways in which I was taught. Please forgive me for repeating a small amount of material from my book *Huna: Ancient Hawaiian Secrets for Modern Living*.

THE PRINCIPLES AS PROVERBS

Uncle William used Hawaiian sparingly while training me, because at that time there were only an estimated two thousand speakers in the whole world, and he decided that speaking it fluently was not necessary for what he wanted to teach me. On the other hand, there were certain concepts that could be grasped more easily as translations of Hawaiian thought. The proverbial sayings below, which I have incorporated into my novel *Dangerous Journeys*, are from him.

1. *Ola i ka mea nui, ola i ka mea iki*: Life is in big things, life is in little things.
2. *Ana 'ole, ke ao, ka po*: The inner world and the outer world are without limit.
3. *No'ono'o ke ali'i, ehu ka ukali*: Thought is the chief, activity is the follower (he loved to do variations on this form).
4. *Noho ka mana i ka Manawa*: Power resides in the present moment (grammatically, it should have been *i keia manawa*, but that's not how Uncle said it).
5. *Ke aloha, ke alo, ke oha, ka ha*: Love is being in the presence of someone or something, sharing joy, giving life.
6. *Mai ka po mai ka mana*: Power comes from the inner world.
7. *Ana 'oia i ka hopena*: Truth is measured by results.

To show that these ideas were not limited to the Kahili family, here are seven proverbs from the book *'Olelo No'eau: Hawaiian Proverbs and Poetical Sayings* by Mary Kawena Pukui (Bishop Museum Press, 1986). They represent only a few of the proverbs and sayings that incorporate the ideas in the principles, but they do show that the ancient Hawaiians were very aware of the seven principles in their own terms.

1. *'A'ohe pau ka 'ike i ka halau ho'okahi*: All knowledge is not taught in one school (a variation on the idea that

there are many sources of knowledge and many ways to think about things).

2. *'A'ohe pu'u ki'eki'e ke ho'a'o 'ia e pi'i*: No hill is too high to be climbed (a way of saying that nothing is impossible and that there are no limits).

3. *He makau hala 'ole*: A fishhook that never fails to catch (said of one who always gets what he wants; the fishhook was a primary symbol of concentrated attention, and a good fishhook was believed capable of attracting fish even without bait).

4. *E pane'e ka wa'a oi moe ka 'ale*: Do it now! (The actual translation is "Set the canoes moving while the waves are at rest.")

5. *He 'olina leo ka ke aloha*: Joy is in the voice of love. (The relationship is obvious.)

6. *Aia no i ka mea e mele ana*: Let the singer select the song. (A poetic way of acknowledging that power comes from within.)

7. *'Ike 'ia no ka loea i ke kuahu*: An expert is recognized by the altar he builds. (As Pukui puts it, "It is what one does and how well he does it that shows whether he is an expert." This is a good guideline for recognizing experts in any field, as well as a good example of the seventh principle. My uncle also liked to use the proverb, *Hö a'e ka 'ike he'enalu i ka hokua o ka 'ale*, "Show your knowledge of surfing on the back of a wave," to illustrate this principle.)

25

THE PRINCIPLES IN STORIES

I have loved stories of nearly any kind ever since my father taught me to read at the age of three, but my favorites have always been myths, legends, and fantasy tales. Perhaps my Uncle William sensed this, or perhaps it was his usual way of teaching. At any rate, he told me lots of stories related to the principles of Huna. Some of these were traditional Hawaiian tales using the traditional storyteller's art of making the story serve the purpose of the telling, and some were Hawaiian versions of tales told elsewhere in the world, whose origin is uncertain. I'll present, in abbreviated form, seven tales, each offering a particular understanding of the principle to which it relates. These stories all feature Maui Kupua, the archetypal hero and shaman famous throughout the Pacific; and because my uncle's original home was Kauai, that is where the tales take place.

WHAT YOU SEE IS WHAT YOU GET

On a beautiful, calm day, Maui paddled an outrigger canoe full of coconuts into the Great Lagoon that used to exist west of the village of Waimea on Kauai. At that time, it was the practice of the High Chief to station a *luna 'auhau*, a sort of customs agent, at the entrance of the lagoon to collect taxes on goods from all who entered for the purpose of trade. So, as Maui paddled up, he was directed to land on the shore before going on. Maui complied with a big smile, and the agent was immediately suspicious, because Maui had a reputation far and wide as a trickster. There was no tax on coconuts, which were plentiful in that land, so the agent, certain that Maui was probably smuggling something, had his boat emptied completely in order to inspect the interior. Nothing was found, however, and Maui was allowed to proceed, although reluctantly. Over the next year, Maui came again about every two months and the same ritual was carried out. The canoe was emptied and searched, each search becoming more and more intensive, until Maui was finally allowed to continue on. After that first year, Maui didn't come anymore, and his trips were mostly forgotten. Many years later, Maui was walking the High Chief's trail from Hanalei in the north to Koloa in the south when he heard someone shout, "*Hele mai 'ai!* Come and eat!" Looking to the side of the path, he saw a man with white hair gesturing for him to join him in front of his hut where he was eating from a bowl of poi. Maui sat with him and shared the poi and they talked politely until the man said, "Maui, do you remember me?" Maui nodded. "I am no longer the High Chief's agent and there is something that has been troubling me all these many years since I saw you last. I know you must have been smuggling something, but I could never figure out what. Please tell me now." Maui took up a large gob of poi, ate it, smacked his lips, smiled, and said, "Canoes."

CHAPTER 2

HOW HIGH CAN YOU GO?

A long, long time ago (at this point some Hawaiian story-tellers like to say, "before Captain Cook"), the sky was very close to the ground, and all human beings had to crawl around on their hands and knees. This was inconvenient, to say the least, and there were a lot of quarrels and bruises when they bumped into each other because their eyes were on the ground. One day Maui, who was crawling around with the rest, bumped into someone and started to get angry, but he was stopped by a very sweet voice. "You're Maui, aren't you?" asked the voice. Maui grumbled assent. "Well, since you're supposed to be a *kupua*, why don't you lift up the sky so we don't have to bump into each other all the time?" Maui bent his head so he could see the speaker, who turned out to be a very pretty young woman. "If you give me a drink from your gourd," he said, "then I'll push up the sky for you" (note: this phrase is usually a meta-phor for something else). The young woman agreed, and so Maui twisted over onto his back and pushed with his feet. Then he knelt and pushed with his shoulders. Then he stood and pushed with his hands. While he was doing so, the mountains, finally freed of the burden of the sky, were growing taller, so Maui climbed them and pushed and pushed until he gave a last great shove and pushed the sky up to where it is today—and that's why we know the story is true. However, some people still never take their eyes off the ground.

KEEP YOUR EYES ON THE GOAL

Maui sailed between the Hawaiian Islands many times and finally decided that they were just too far apart, so he planned to bring them all together. He went to his mother, Hina, to ask for her advice, and she told him that if he could manage to catch the giant fish, *Luehu* (scattered), then he would succeed. She also told him that it was very important for whoever was helping him to keep their eyes on the fish no matter what happened. Maui collected his magic fishhook, *Manaiakalani* (lei needle from heaven), talked his four brothers into helping, and paddled with them out into the deep ocean to find the giant fish (probably a whale). Finding Luehu, Maui caught it with his hook. The whale took them on a wild ride around the ocean in a big circle, causing the fishing line to wrap around the islands, and at last Maui's brothers were able to hold the great fish still and draw him toward Kauai, paddling backward for all they were worth. As the great fish (or big whale) was being pulled toward the canoe, the islands were being drawn together as well. Then a canoe bailer floated past Maui's canoe. All the brothers ignored it except the last and youngest one, who just picked it up and tossed it behind him in case it might become useful. As they got closer and closer to the shores of Kauai, the brothers heard loud shouting from the people on shore. The youngest brother turned around and saw that the canoe bailer had turned into a beautiful woman. "Look, brothers!" he shouted, and all the other brothers except Maui turned around and gazed with wonder on the beauty of this magical woman. At that moment, the fishing line broke, the whale escaped, and the islands drifted back to where they were before.

WHERE ARE YOU?

Ever curious about everything, Maui decided to join the priestly order of *Ku* in order to discover what it was all about. Since this order was extremely strict, Maui had to spend lots of time at lectures and in meetings to learn all the rules and regulations. One day Maui, as an acolyte, was told to accompany one of the older priests to a temple some distance away. As they traveled the path, the old priest kept up a steady monologue about the importance of following the rules. Some hours into the journey, they came to a flooded stream, and there on the bank was a young woman with a large load of *tapa* (a bark cloth used for clothes and bedding), weeping bitterly. On seeing the men, she begged them to carry her across so that she could get home before dark, because it was an area where bandits roamed after nightfall. The old priest ignored her completely, and Maui only smiled at her pleasantly without speaking. This was because it was a time of month when priests and acolytes of this order were to have nothing at all to do with women. When the old priest was ready to cross, he ordered Maui to carry him. Maui, being very strong, picked up the priest in one arm and the girl with her bundle in the other and stomped across the stream. There, he put both of them down and began walking onward. The priest hustled up beside him, red with anger. He spoke no word but his face became more and more red, and after a mile he finally broke out with an eruption of abusive words about how Maui had broken the rules. Maui looked at him in surprise and waited until the torrent had stopped. Then, gently, he said, "Are you still carrying that woman? I set her down by the stream."

IN THE SPIRIT OF ALOHA

Long, long ago, when everything was different, Maui found his mother, Hina, crying outside her hut. When he asked her what was wrong, she said that the sun was traveling across the sky so fast her tapa cloth could not dry properly. Like a good son, Maui said he would take care of it. First, Maui taught his brothers how to make cord and, with the cord, how to make nets. They made a big, strong net and took it to the top of the mountain, *Haleakala* (House of the Sun), where the sun came out of his cave every morning to make his journey across the sky. Before dawn, the brothers draped the net over the mouth of the cave and got ready. Morning came, the brothers held the net tight, and the sun burned right through it as if it were paper and went racing on. Realizing that ordinary cord wouldn't work, Maui went to his *kupua* (trickster god) sister, also named Hina, and asked for some of her hair with which to make a net. Since she had magical powers, her hair looked exactly the same even after she had cut off as much as Maui needed. With this hair, Maui and his brothers made a new net and climbed the mountain again, draping the net over the cave once more and waiting for dawn. When it was time, the sun burst out of the cave, but this time he was held by the magical net of hair. He was able to rise just high enough to shine onto the plains where the people lived, but there he was held fast in spite of terrific struggles. About midday it was getting very hot. Maui was both elated with his success and troubled by what he was going to do next, especially when his mother appeared and told him that this wasn't going to work because everything in the villages was burning up. Finally, Maui's grandmother, also named Hina, suggested that they do a *ho'oponopono* (a traditional kind of reconciliation process) with the sun. Maui got the sun to sit down with all the people, and together they aired their grievances and offered solutions. The outcome was that the sun agreed to go more slowly across the sky for half the year, and the people agreed that the sun could go more quickly during the other half. That is the way it is today, and so we know the story is true. We also know the story is true because sometimes you can still see the strands of Maui's magical net hanging down from the sun through the clouds.

THE SECRET OF FIRE

A very, very long time ago, human beings had to eat all their food raw because only the *'alae* (mud hen) birds had the secret of fire, and they guarded it jealously. One day Maui gagged on some raw meat and complained to his mother, Hina, and she told him he would have to get the secret of fire from the 'alae birds if he wanted cooked food. So Maui went to the swampy area by the Waimea River, where those birds lived, and tried to sneak up on them while they were gathered around their fire. But the birds were too quick for him. They scratched out the fire and scattered all the embers before he could catch either them or a piece of burning wood. Time after time, Maui tried with no success, so he went back to his mother and asked for advice. Hina suggested he try to catch the youngest bird late at night when they were all sleepy. This Maui could do. After catching the youngest bird, he choked him until he agreed to give up the secret. First the bird said that the secret was to rub two pieces of taro stalk together. Maui was no fool, so he held on to the little bird while rubbing pieces of taro together. When it didn't work because the taro stalks were too soft, Maui choked the bird even harder. So the bird told him the secret was to rub two *ti-plant* stalks together, but when Maui tried that—still holding onto the bird—it didn't work either, for the same reason. Furious, Maui almost squeezed the life out of the little bird, who finally squawked, "Fire is in the water." Maui was so surprised that he loosened his hold and the bird escaped. Maui realized that he had been given a riddle, and as he was a great lover of riddles, he decided to figure it out rather than try to catch the bird again. After many days, Maui figured out that *Waimea*, the name of the river, means "red water," and that this is also a nickname for the hardwood tree, *olomea*. In addition, the yellow blossoms of the *hau*, a softwood tree that grows along the banks of the river, turn red in the evening and fall onto the water. Finally, he recalled that the phrase *wai'ula 'ili ahi* (red water with a surface of fire) is a poetic name for the Waimea River on Kauai. Putting this all together, he rubbed a piece of hau with a piece of olomea and produced fire. Before sharing his discovery with his people, Maui caught the young mud hen again and hit it on the head with a burning stick to teach it a lesson. And we know this is true because all Hawaiian mud hens today have a big red patch on their heads.

THERE'S ALWAYS ANOTHER WAY TO DO ANYTHING

'Awa (known elsewhere as *kava*) is a plant the ancient Hawaiians used for a sacred drink by crushing and boiling the roots to make a mildly narcotic tea. Far back in the olden days, however, the secret of making the 'awa drink was kept by the god Kane (pronounced "kah-nay").

Every time the people wanted to do a ceremony, they had to send a man to Kane's floating island and beg for some. This went on for a long time, until one day Maui was chosen to go and get the 'awa. When he arrived in the presence of Kane, the young kupua was upset to find that he had to beg and grovel until Kane was ready to turn his back, make the drink, and then turn back around and hand over a single bowl. Maui acted very humble and gave his thanks and left, but before leaving the island he managed to trip over a tree root and spill all the drink on the ground. He went back to Kane and asked for more, begging and groveling with even greater humility until Kane made it again and gave him a new bowl. Maui managed to spill this one, too, and two more as well, until Kane, in his haste to get rid of this bothersome human, made the 'awa drink without turning around, and Maui could see how it was done. Maui thanked the god profusely, promising to be extremely careful this time, and departed with glee. Since then, no man has had to ask Kane for his bowl of 'awa.

I wish to make one more comment before we plunge deeply into the art and practice of changing reality. Throughout the book I may incorporate experiences that I have written about before. Please be tolerant and realize that I am using them to illustrate specific concepts in the context of a specific chapter. I will do my best either to expand or shorten the story, whichever I believe serves you best.

Part 2

Changing Reality in the Objective World

Remember

Remember what it's like to wake up smiling,
Remember what it's like to feel so good,
Remember when your heart felt so much lighter,
Better than you ever thought it could.

When skies are dark and gray the sun's still shining,
It doesn't even matter if it rains,
When things don't turn out right just keep on going,
Let laughter take away the aches and pains.

(Chorus)
Let's have a party,
Let's have some fun;
Invite our friends, and everyone.
We'll do some healing
The Hawaiian way,
We'll have a party
And then we'll play.

So keep those memories of love alive and kicking,
Recall the times you used to dance and sing;
Be here and now with all the good you can remember,
Then go ahead and do your healing thing.

—Serge Kahili King, 2001

Chapter 3

Knowledge Can Be Power

W hen I first moved to Kauai many years ago to set up a center for teaching and healing, my colleagues and I took great pleasure in exploring the island's many hiking trails. We crossed and recrossed streams and rivers, trekked long sandy beaches, climbed hills and mountains, and explored forests and swamps. We learned the names of some trees and plants and waterfalls and peaks, studied Hawaiian history and culture, and thought ourselves fairly knowledgeable, which we were when compared to *malihinis,* "newcomers." We traveled some areas so frequently that we almost considered ourselves experts on those places. And then one weekend we were pleasantly shocked into a whole new state of awareness.

LEARNING TO LEARN

On the weekend I just mentioned, the three of us took a course from a young Hawaiian man who had dedicated himself to the study and re-creation of the ancient Hawaiian art of stone carving. We learned how various tools were made, and we were even given a project of making stone bowls. The most enlightening part of the course, however, was a field trip during which we were taught how to recognize broken adzes, hammerstones, and files, not just from the teacher's collection, but lying around in plain sight along roadways, on beaches, and in streams. We were also shown how to notice when larger stones and boulders had been modified by stone tools. It may sound like it was just an interesting course for an archeology buff, but I have to tell you that the knowledge I gained that weekend profoundly changed my experience of Kauai and my experience of life in general. When I walked the trails, I could tell when I was walking in the footsteps of the former inhabitants, whereas before I was just walking on a trail with stones on it. Crossing streams became a way of learning where and how the ancients had worked. Sitting on beach boulders became a way of knowing where the gathering places of fishermen and stone workers had been. Most of all, though, the experience greatly increased my ability to be more aware of my surroundings, no matter where I was, and to use that awareness in productive ways. Sometimes I even felt a bit of kinship with Sherlock Holmes.

THE MYTH OF MATTER

There are people so habitually oriented to first-level assumptions that they make it a matter of pride to say things like, "I only believe what I can see or touch." With a little prodding, they would probably add "hear" and "taste." It sounds substantial until you learn more about human physiology. I discuss this subject in detail in my book *Healing Relationships*, so I will write about it here only briefly.

When you see, touch, hear, or taste something, you are not really doing that at all. The physiological fact is that all your sensory impressions are indirect experiences of reality. Light waves from objects are sorted by elements in your eyes and converted into electrical impulses that are sent to your brain, where they are inexplicably (meaning that not a single scientist knows how it happens) transformed into apparent awareness of an object or a color. The same is true of sound waves, pressure against the skin, and impressions from taste buds. If you believe only what you can see or touch, then you believe only what insubstantial electrical impulses are telling you. When you add to that truth the scientific finding that solid matter is in fact only mostly empty space, then priding yourself on being a hard-headed realist because you rely on your physical senses for determining what is real begins to seem a little silly.

However, that kind of scientifically based view of first-level reality isn't very practical for everyday life, so let's ignore it for now and move on.

CHAPTER 3

FIRST-LEVEL CHANGE

When people want to change reality in the objective world, they usually think in terms of physical hands or physical tools to move things, modify things, put things together, or to make or invent other things to do those tasks. Also included in this effort is organizing and teaching people to do those things. In order to move beyond the minimum required for subsistence living, though, you need knowledge that can help you do all those things better. I am reminded of the old story of a repairman who was hired to fix a furnace. He went down into the basement of a house, followed closely by the owner, and inspected the furnace for a while. Then he hit it once with a hammer and it started working again. When he presented a bill for one hundred dollars, the owner was outraged. "Why, I could have done that," he complained. "I think you'd better re-do that bill." So the repairman made up another bill that said, "Hitting the furnace with a hammer—$10. Knowing where to hit—$90."

Of course, everyone has to gain some knowledge in order to do anything skillfully. But it has been my experience that the majority of people learn only what they need to earn the kind of living they want. And they get so comfortable with what they know that they don't bother to learn more unless it is forced on them, often with great resistance on their part. This tendency, in turn, greatly limits their ability to change their own reality.

Here is an example: Many of my readers know that I developed a first-level, objective world, self-healing technique called "Dynamind." It uses simple, common knowledge of breathing, muscle relaxation, and stimulation of circulation, but it organizes these elements in a way that produces exceptionally fast relief from pain and other physical and emotional symptoms, including some that are not generally considered to be treatable. Although the process lies completely within the realm of conventional healing, the application and results are so unusual that many people have a strong resistance to accepting or believing their own experience of relief. As a result, they either refuse to use it again or desperately try to recreate the symptoms in order to use a treatment that fits, in their minds, the way a healing is "supposed" to happen.

Recently I was teaching Dynamind to a group of senior citizens. One woman who had broken her toe three months before and was still having strong pain whenever she walked took part in a demonstration. In less than two minutes she could walk normally because the pain was completely gone. Another woman had some strong emotional hurt about a relationship. It took about five minutes for her to feel relief and be able to think about the person in a calm way. Yet, in spite of these dramatic demonstrations, some members of the audience refused to participate and even gave the instructions back.

So obtaining increased knowledge in itself is not sufficient to enable someone to change reality. You have to *use* the knowledge in some way to turn it into creative power. Otherwise, it is merely information.

DYNAMIC DENDRITES

Although it was thought for a long time that the brain was merely an organ designed for memory storage and recall, recent research indicates that the brain is much more dynamic than that, constantly changing and growing according to our behavior.

Many modern brain researchers are concentrating on a particular part of a neuron, a nerve cell, called a dendrite. Picture the main part of a neuron as being like the trunk of a tree. Dendrites, then, are the branches. In simplified terms, these branches connect with the branches of other neurons to share information. The more branches, the more sharing of information.

It is known that dendrites, the branches, will increase in number as a person's environment becomes richer in sensory experience. This includes, apparently, things like travel to new places, learning new skills, and new mental experiences that stimulate the imagination. It is also known that excessive alcohol consumption will inhibit dendrite growth, and that senility (now usually called dementia) is associated with an actual loss of dendrites. Some researchers propose that a decrease in sensory stimulation contributes to senility, which is characterized largely by difficulty in learning new things and more frequently by forgetting recent events. In addition to certain diseases, other factors leading to senility, and decreased dendrites, may include emotional trauma, over-medication, dehydration, vitamin deficiencies, and excessive use of drugs, as well as the aforementioned alcohol. The possibility also exists that when you stop learning, your dendrites stop growing and start to fade away.

Theoretically, the more dendrites you have, the more creative you will be, the more idea associations you will make, and the more easily you will learn new skills. All of this translates, of course, into more potential for changing your reality.

Theories aside, what is known for a fact is that the more new things you learn, and the more new experiences you have, the more ability you have to change your reality. *If* . . .

The big *If* refers to one more factor. Remember the stories of the furnace repairman and the senior citizens in my workshop? New knowledge by itself doesn't automatically translate into new power. The additional factor required is motivation. It is when you want to do, be, or have something that new knowledge, new experiences, and new skills—no matter what they are—create associations that stimulate ideas for creating what you want and generate the mental, emotional, and physical energy to do it.

THE LEGACY OF LANGUAGE

The language you grew up with carries with it a hidden legacy of assumptions about reality that permeate your life. Depending on the language and how you use it, these assumptions can inhibit your creativity in some areas and expand it in others. Since English is my native language, let's start with it as an example.

In some ways, English can be an incredibly creative language and one that stimulates and eases the way to creativity. I believe that this is largely due to its essentially "pidgin" nature. A pidgin language is generally considered to be a grammatically simplified language developed between people without a common language. Hawaiian pidgin developed this way among Hawaiian, Chinese, Japanese, Korean, Anglo, Portuguese, and Filipino laborers.

Students of English often forget that it developed as a pidgin language among Angles, Saxons, French, and Scandinavians. Later, English proved its flexibility by easily incorporating words in most of the language groups from the rest of the world, words that found their way into English dictionaries. Just now, hardly trying, I looked up five originally Hawaiian words that are now part of the English language. Not content with borrowing whole words for new concepts, English also contains many words that are made-up constructions from other languages, such as Greek and Latin. And then there is English slang, composed of entirely new words or old words given new meaning.

English also has several specialized forms, the most impressive of which, in my opinion, is poetry. In poetry, a certain idea can be said in a different way, breaking rules of grammar and logical thought, in order to allow for new imagery, feelings, and creative potential. Here is a small example:

> Prose: I have a cherry tree that is in bloom, and it is so
> beautiful that it reminds me of someone I love.

> Poetry: A cherry tree have I
> With flowers in its hair
> And branches slim and firm
> So like my lady fair

Not great poetry, I admit, but that's not the point. The point is that each statement about the same thing, said in a different way, produces a different experience.

Now, after raving about English, we need to examine its limitations. One is that it is not a very emotionally evocative language when words alone are used. Some emotional excitement can be aroused when certain words are yelled, and sometimes the right phrase said at the right time can stir people up, but the written word is relatively flat compared to the effects that other languages can produce. For example, I read *The Three Musketeers* by Alexander Dumas in English and thoroughly enjoyed it. Then I read it in French and laughed and cried out loud.

A different kind of limitation comes from the English verb *to be*. While extremely useful in some ways, it carries a presumption of existence and identification that often interferes with creativity. For instance, the English sentence "I am angry" not only expresses the existence of anger, it also creates an identification between the speaker and the descriptive adverb. Many times in my healing work, the stumbling block in a client's progress comes from this kind of identification, whether it originated with the client or with someone who criticized the client. In a similar vein, a statement like "the situation is hopeless" does more than just describe the situation. It creates an identification of the situation with hopelessness, which too often results in the speaker not even trying to change it. Interestingly, there is an experimental form of English called "E-Prime" that tries to use English without the verb *to be*, but it has encountered a lot of difficulties. However, languages like Russian, Indonesian, and Hawaiian do very well without the verb *to be*.

Almost as problematic as the verb *to be* is the tendency for Indo-European languages to turn intangible experiences into nouns, which leads us to think and act as if the intangible experience were an objectively physical thing. One of the best examples is "pain." Pain is a real experience, but it is not a real thing. Because it has been "thingified" (turned into a noun), however, we talk about "getting rid of pain" as if it were something that could be taken out of the body like a nail; we talk about "pain moving around" in the body, as if it were some kind of insect under the skin that moves to another location when we try to "get rid of it"; and we talk about pain "coming back" after it has been relieved, as if it were some kind of living entity that just went on vacation for a while before returning to hurt us. This kind of thinking is part of what makes pain so difficult to treat. Treating pain as an effect, on the other hand, makes it very easy to relieve, because then all you have to do is to change the behavior that produces the effect. Another example might help make this clearer. We also talk about ocean waves as if they were objective things, yet at the same time we know that they are only the effect of wind or earth movement. When the wind stops blowing or the earth stops moving, waves don't go anywhere; they cease to exist.

Still another limitation, shared by other Indo-European languages, is that English grammar forces you to think in linear terms of past, present, and future. Because of the language structure, the assumption that time is linear by nature is extremely strong throughout the cultures that use this type of structure. Another way of saying this is that past, present, and future are real because our language says they are. Of course, we've managed to engage in a lot of reality changing in spite of that, but what could we do and what could we experience if we thought differently about time?

The Hawaiian language, by comparison, does not have past, present, and future tenses. It only has verbal markers for completed, ongoing, and potential actions. The English sentence "I went to the store yesterday and bought some eggs" could be translated into Hawaiian, but the real sense of the Hawaiian would be "My going to the store yesterday to buy some eggs is over." The English expresses the experience of an event in the past, while the Hawaiian expresses the experience of an event in the present. Likewise, the English "I will go to the store tomorrow to buy some eggs" expresses action in a future time, while the Hawaiian equivalent, "My going to the store tomorrow hasn't happened yet," again expresses an experience of the present.

And the point is . . . ? Only that our presumption of a real past and a real future automatically guides our thoughts and actions in certain ways, and a presumption of a dominant present moment might open up other possibilities of thoughts and actions. For instance, many people could change their reality more easily if they could stop thinking of the past as a burden they had to keep carrying with them and start thinking of the past as recordings stored in memories that exist in the present. And they wouldn't have to speak Hawaiian to make that shift. Just knowing there is another way to think about it can make a difference.

THE SE FACTOR

In the objective world, as in all the others, it is critically important to consider the SE factor. "SE" stands for Self-Esteem. I know that this subject has been repeatedly discussed by many people. Nevertheless, I must emphasize that the art and skill of changing reality is highly dependent on it, because from self-esteem comes self-confidence, and from self-confidence comes decisive action to create positive change.

Fundamentally, self-esteem is merely the way you think about yourself in relation to the world around you. The more you think of yourself as worthwhile, deserving, competent, and empowered to follow your purpose, the easier it is to change reality at the First Level, on your own and through interaction with other people.

Constantly affirming your self-esteem is good, as is refusing to doubt your worth and your right to make changes. However, I have found that three other often-neglected things are immensely useful as supporting behaviors. They are energy, strength, and posture.

Having abundant physical energy helps you feel good, not only in your body, but about yourself. In the objective world, physical energy can be increased without effort by regular relaxation, deeper breathing, and good hydration (drinking enough water). Various people propose many other methods of increasing physical energy, but none are as universally effective as those just mentioned.

Closely related to physical energy is physical strength. Some ways of changing reality in the objective world, like construction work and athletic performance, require physical strength, but my point is that physical strength also increases self-esteem, with all of its benefits. You may or may not want to hear this, but the single most effective way to increase physical strength is exercise. Massive muscle-building or grueling endurance tests are not necessary, but do them if you like them. Even something as simple as walking more can be a great help. In addition to physical strength, there is mental strength to consider. There's no mystery about mental strength. All it takes to increase mental strength is the decision to do something and then doing it, without letting distractions or difficulties stop you. And if the way you try to accomplish it doesn't work, just change your plans and do it differently. Whether you apply this to some vast global project or to cleaning the house doesn't matter. Every time you use mental strength, you increase your self-esteem and your reality-changing abilities.

Posture directly affects your mental state, your emotional state, and your physical state. People usually think it is the other way around—acknowledging that thoughts, emotions, and health affect your posture. Yes, that's true, but it works the other way, too. By practicing confident postures in relation to your daily activities you can clear your mind, calm your emotions, improve your health, and increase your self-esteem.

OBJECTIVE-WORLD TECHNIQUES FOR CHANGING REALITY

1. Learn more about what you already know. Here is one exercise for doing so that has many possible variations:
   a. Stand in sunlight and seek to learn something new about the way sunlight affects you or your environment. For example, does it warm all parts of your

body equally? Does it make sharp edges to shadows, or fuzzy ones?

b. Stand in the wind. Does it feel the same all over your body? Does it move like a steady flow, or does it move in waves or ripples?

c. Look at and touch the bark of several trees. How are they different?

d. Try this technique with other things in nature, in your home, in your office. What can you discover that you didn't know before?

2. Play a game of "This Reminds Me of Myself."

a. With a partner, pick up any object and describe how it reminds you of yourself.

b. Example: Right now I am sitting at my desk writing this book, and I have just picked up a key. It reminds me of myself because it is designed to unlock something, and that's what I do with my studies and teaching. It is round and smooth where you hold it, and that's the smooth exterior I present to people. The part that goes inside the lock is more complicated; it is like the tools and techniques I use to help people open up. The hole it has for a key ring is like the openings I give people to connect with me. And this particular key opens a treasure box, like the different possibilities that I open up for people. See? It's easy and fun, and it's creative.

3. Play a game of "What if?" Think of something that is obviously true or obviously the way it is supposed

to be, and ask yourself, "What if it were different? How would that change things?" Here are some examples: What if the past really didn't exist? What if doors were windows and windows were doors? What if the automobile had never been invented but airplanes had? What if everyone spoke the same language?

4. To stimulate dendritic connections, sit and think about how something in your life could be improved. Don't "try" to think about it. Just let yourself wonder.

5. Perform a task, any task, with full conscious involvement of all your senses, especially sight, sound, and touch. Be sure to include full conscious awareness of your body as you do the task. This will help you to increase your general awareness, improve your skills, and discover new ways to act that will make you feel better.

6. Practice increasing your self-esteem by increasing your energy, strengthening your body and mind, and consciously changing your posture.

Part 3

Changing Reality in the Subjective World

I Am Loved

The birds and bees love me,
The trees love me,
And all the fishes swimming
In the seas love me;
I know that
All of Nature loves me, too.

Yes, the Moon loves me,
The sun at noon loves me,
And the stars that are coming
Out soon love me;
I'm happy 'cause
The Universe loves me, too.

The spirits of Fire, Wind, and Stone love me,
And the spirit of Water feels the same;
My furred and feathered, scaled and naked
Friends all love me,
So do people who don't even know my name.

I hope that you love me,
Say you do love me,
Speak right up and tell me that it's
True you love me,
And I'll tell you that
I love you, too.

—Serge Kahili King, 1987

Chapter 4

ESP—You Can't Live without It

⌒

When we are dealing with ideas related to the subjective world, the acronym ESP is often used to describe the abilities associated with it. Usually, the letters *ESP* are taken to stand for the words, *extra-sensory perception*. This is based on an objective-world assumption that the abilities used, such as telepathy, clairvoyance, and psycho-kinesis, are somehow beyond or outside of our so-called "physical" senses. I strongly disagree with this. For that reason, I prefer to interpret ESP as meaning "extended sensory perception/projection." And to describe the people who use their senses in this way with conscious intent, I will borrow a term from science fiction and call them "espers."

If you believe that espers are unique individuals who were born with or have somehow received a special gift that sets them apart from other human beings; or that esper abilities are a sort of reward for moral purity (what-ever that means); or that years of intense and arduous effort and practice are necessary before esper abilities will ever appear, then you and millions like you have been victims of some of the greatest hoaxes ever suffered by the human race.

The truth is that every man, woman, and child on this planet is an esper, in the sense of having the abilities to perform all the feats associated with metaphysical talents. These are not even primitive abilities that have been lost or atrophied as man has become more civilized (whatever that means). These abilities are alive and well and kicking inside you at this moment.

The only differences between you and a conscious esper are these: The esper pays more attention to feelings and sensations that you ignore. The esper has learned, through trial and error or by training, how to stimulate such feelings and sensations and how to discriminate among them. Finally, the esper trusts these feelings and sensations and believes in the actuality of what is being done, and he or she practices accordingly.

I know what I am talking about for two reasons: first, I was trained by my father and others, and I trained myself as well to demonstrate almost every form of esper ability; second, I have trained thousands of others to do the same. The people I trained were just ordinary humans like you who were reasonably skeptical in the beginning, but in all my courses on esper development, every one of my students demonstrated the esper abilities being taught to some degree. Contrary to common thinking, most of these abilities can be experienced after only a half-hour or less of training. It takes more time to convince someone that it can be done than to show them how to do it. And naturally, it takes time on the part of the student to become skilled. You can learn how to hold a golf club and hit a ball in a few minutes, but it takes practice to become good at it. And one other thing: just as you can learn golf from a golf expert without the need for a special, secret ritual to open up your "golf center," so can you learn esper abilities from an esper expert without the need for secret rituals.

The biggest problem facing people interested in developing their natural esper talents is that they don't know what the experience is supposed to feel like. In our culture, esper powers are generally considered to be so alien to the normal way of doing things that people tend to expect sensations totally different from what they are used to. In reality, most of the sensations are so much the same as normal experiences that people may have a tough time accepting that what they already do differs only slightly from what the experienced espers do.

You still have doubts as to whether you might be an esper? Let's see whether any of your experiences fit into the following categories of obvious and not so obvious esper experiences. Have you ever

- had a hunch that turned out right?
- had an intuitive feeling about something that turned out to be accurate?

59

- had a dream that came true, even in part?
- thought of someone and, shortly after, received a telephone call from them?
- called someone who told you they had just thought of you?
- picked up the phone to call someone only to find them already on the line?
- thought of someone and received a letter from them within a few days?
- shared the same dream with someone else?
- seen a vision or apparition of a close friend or relative who was in trouble, near death, or already passed on?
- had a daydream that came true?
- experienced déja vu, the feeling that you had been in a place or experienced a situation before?
- said the same thing at the same time as someone else?
- wished hard that someone would do a certain thing and then they did it?
- stared at someone consciously or unconsciously and had them turn around to look at you?
- been the recipient of such a stare and turned around yourself?
- avoided a trip of any kind during which there was an accident?
- driven your car while your mind was occupied and failed to remember having driven as far as you did?
- had a sudden feeling or anxiety about a child who turned out to need your presence?

• felt uncomfortable in a given place for no apparent reason?
• walked on fire with no harm?

The above list could be extended a great deal, but if you have ever experienced anything similar to the above, you definitely have esper talent. Even if you haven't experienced any of these things, I still claim that you are inherently esper just because you are human, but you'll have to prove that for yourself by trying out the experiences given in the rest of part two.

SIXTH-SENSE NONSENSE

Researchers who are looking for a "sixth sense" or more to explain esper phenomena are wasting their time. "Extrasensory Perception" is a misnomer, a term that is highly misleading. Esper abilities are merely extensions of your common, everyday, garden-variety type of senses. That's why I use the term "Extended Sensory Perception/ Projection." Whether it is realized or not, a skilled esper is just a person who has refined his regular sensory awareness to the point where he notices what others don't; he has learned to correctly interpret what his senses are telling him.

Curiously, there are many respectable professions in which this type of ability is used, only we don't call it esper. As an example, suppose someone offers you a glass of vintage wine. Most likely you will take a sip and pronounce it good or bad. If you fancy yourself a connoisseur, you might sniff it first, make a statement about its "bouquet," or roll some of it on your tongue and declare it "smooth," "dry," or "young." And that's about it. A professional wine taster, on the other hand, after sniffing, looking, tasting, and swallowing, can tell you what kind of grape was used, whether or not it is a blend, possibly where and when it was grown and what kind of soil it was grown in, maybe even the amount of rainfall the grapes received, and what it will taste like five, ten, or twenty years from now. In short, the taster has demonstrated the esper abilities of psychometry, clairvoyance, and prophesy. But unless he went on to describe your wine rack at home and state whether or not you would buy a bottle, we wouldn't ordinarily call him an esper. And yet, the difference is only the area toward which the abilities are directed.

BODY MIND AND FOCUS MIND

In order to help you develop your esper abilities to the utmost, I am going to give you a concept that comes from Huna. Whether it is scientifically acceptable or not doesn't matter. The point is that it works.

According to this idea, you have two minds. One we can call the body mind, and it is in charge of all the involuntary processes of your body, including the receiving and storing of all information that comes through your senses. In a way, you can compare it to the subconscious or the right side of your brain, but it is really more than either of those. So just think of it as the body mind. The other mind we will call the focus mind. This is "you," the part of you that is aware of being conscious (which means "aware of being aware"). I call it the focus mind because, like an adjustable flashlight, it focuses on only a part of what the senses are telling it at any given time, even though that focus can be widened or narrowed. For example, if you are watching a movie, your attention may be focused on the film and nothing else. But you could expand your focus to include the taste of popcorn in your mouth, the feel of your companion's hand in yours, and the heavy breathing of the guy next to you. If you expanded your focus further to include the people in the seats in front of you, the curtains by the side of the screen, the various grunts and coughs and sniffles of the audience, and the discomfort of your chair, you would probably begin to lose your focus on the movie. And you would probably not be paying any attention to the sensations of your clothing on your skin, the temperature and smell of the air, and sundry other things that your body mind is making available to you through your senses.

When developing ESP, it is convenient to think of your body mind as an employee, the supervisor in direct charge of your physical body, your sense organs, and your energy level. As the focus mind, you are the manager of the whole operation. Some people even like to give the body mind a nickname as a means of establishing closer rapport and communication. In terms of ESP, we will be most concerned with the senses. The whole of your sensory system can be effectively thought of as a radio-television receiver/transmitter run by the body mind. The ordinary sensory signals—like the sights, sounds, tastes, touches, and smells that clearly have a physical source—can be compared to AM radio and VHF broadcast television channels, and the ESP part of your equipment can be compared to FM radio and UHF channels on TV. In reality, the differences aren't so clear cut, but this model will serve to get you started.

Chapter 5

The Telepathic Connection

The word *telepathy* means "sensing at a distance," and, in its broadest meaning, it covers all forms of ESP. Telepathy is basic to the human race, and it is doubtful whether we could survive without it, even in this day and age. Not only does it help all of us in times of danger, but it provides the link for group and community effort and is highly important in maintaining and passing on cultural knowledge. No strictly mechanical theory of learning can explain how a child can learn all it does to survive and sustain itself as a human being in a given culture. Telepathic transmission of knowledge is a fact and a necessity.

In teaching you to develop your telepathic abilities, however, we will use the more limited definition of telepathy as "direct, internal, mind-to-mind communication." Otherwise, we will overlap into clairvoyance, psychometry, astral travel, and other forms of ESP. Fundamentally, they are all forms of telepathy, but they are easier to teach and to learn when they are classified separately. One thing to remember is that we are using a Huna concept that everything has a "mind" to communicate with.

WHY BOTHER TO LEARN TELEPATHY?

Since you're reading this book, I assume you've already resolved the question of the benefit of telepathy, but let's look at the practical side anyway.

Apart from the potential satisfaction of being able to wow an audience, consciously controlled telepathy will allow you to become far more aware of your surroundings and the people in them, and this information can help you to be more effective in all areas of life. By understanding telepathy better, you will be less affected by the prevailing moods and emotions around you, and you will be able to project better moods to others. If you have pets, you will be able to call them when you want them, even if they have wandered out of sight. More useful, perhaps, will be the ability to call your spouse or children to dinner without moving from your chair. If you have to meet someone in an airport or in a large amusement park, you can do so with a minimum of fuss and worry. If you have business dealings with someone, you can get a good indication of their intentions through telepathy. And if you want to help people or animals or the environment, telepathy is an effective way to do it. Your own imagination can probably supply you with many more possible uses. And those mentioned are not just pleasant fantasies. They are practiced now successfully by people who thought they had no telepathic ability to begin with. Finally, whether or not you wish to think of this as practical, increasing your telepathic ability is a major step to increasing your total awareness and effectiveness in every area of life, and, no less importantly, for changing reality.

ESP AND ENERGY

The Huna approach I mentioned previously includes the idea that the effectiveness of esper abilities depends a great deal on the amount of energy a person has available. This is a particular type of energy that goes by many names, such as "life force," *prana, chi, ki,* and a host of others (the Hawaiian word *mana* is not included because it means something different). Simply put, it is the energy that makes you alive. It is also the energy that powers your sensory equipment. The more power a radio/television transmitter has, the more distant signals it can pick up and the farther it can transmit. Your own system works in much the same way.

When you are fatigued, depressed, or under tension, your esper energy is restricted or blocked. Then it is like trying to operate a radio or television with weak batteries or during a brownout. On the other hand, when you are relaxed and in a good mood, the power flows easily and your abilities are sharper. This is one of the reasons for increasingly poor results in ESP testing labs the longer the tests are run. The poor subjects simply get tired of doing it. Fortunately, there are ways of building up your flow of esper energy above and beyond what you have even when you are feeling good. With the greater amount of esper energy, you can get even better results with all forms of ESP.

I am going to recommend a very easy way to increase your flow of esper energy that anyone can use. This will already be familiar to students of Huna and readers of my other books, but I'll present it here for anyone else who might find it useful. A more advanced form will be given in the techniques section later:

1. Inhale with your attention on the crown of your head.
2. Exhale with your attention on your navel.
3. Keep this up for at least a minute.

If you are a reasonably normal person, you will find after doing this exercise with your eyes closed that your body will be more relaxed, your vision will be clearer, colors will look brighter, and your hearing will be sharper. So think of what it must do for your FM and UHF senses. Yes, this exercise will also increase the amount of oxygen in your blood, but it will bring in something else from the atmosphere as well (and I'm not talking about smog).

On a clear day, or at least when the sky looks blue, stand with your back to the sun and focus your gaze about ten or twenty feet in front of you into the sky. If you see floating black hair-like or cell-like objects, pay no attention. Those are on your eyeballs. Just keep gazing and soon you will see a mass of spinning, twirling, popping things that look like whitish commas, dots, and dashes. I'll bet they never showed you that in high school—or college, either. Those strange objects have been called energy globules or orgone vesicles by others. I call them "vril drops" and they are in the air, not on your eye. When you breathe deeply, that's the energy you are adding to your system.

For many other ways to increase esper energy, I recommend my book *Earth Energies*. From now on I will assume that you will charge yourself up with esper energy before practicing any of the esper exercises given later in this book.

TYPES OF TELEPATHY

Telepathy is easier to understand and to learn when we break it down into various types. The two major categories are Receiving and Sending. Each one has its own technique and special problems. Both of these categories can be broken down further into Passive (involuntary) and Active (voluntary) forms. And, as you might have guessed, each of these can be broken down further. We'll start out with the receiving type of telepathy.

Passive Telepathic Receiving

In this section we will cover empathetic (or emotional) telepathy and intellectual telepathy—including the important topic of telepathic neutrality.

Empathetic Telepathy

Empathetic Telepathy is received on an emotional or feeling level. Many people unconsciously use this type of telepathy with animals and very small children. Such people "instinctively" understand the needs and wants of animals and/or children and are able to respond accurately to them without speaking a word. Of course, familiar gestures and body language play a role here, but so does true telepathy. If you have ever met a person you immediately liked—or disliked—without reason, then you have been using telepathy whether you realized it or not. Children, whose minds are generally less blocked than those of adults, are often excellent judges of character because of their telepathic ability to pick up a person's true intentions, even when all the adults around them have been fooled.

Adults are not completely out of it, however. Telepathy is at work whenever you pick up another person's mood, be it one of elation or depression. When a group of people have the same general train of thought on an emotional level it can quickly spread to others around them. This is why some parties are great fun and others are dull, even though the same people may attend both occasions. This is also what turns a crowd into a mob, and it is why innocent bystanders can find themselves caught up in the mob fever without knowing what happened. I'd like to give a personal example of the last case. When I was younger and less aware, I happened to be attending the University of Michigan during a campaign visit by Richard Nixon. Politically I was neutral, but I wanted to see what he had to say. So I followed along the edge of a massive crowd parading down the streets to greet him . . . ending up only twenty feet from his podium. There were ten thousand supporters there, the papers reported later. Toward the end of his speech, I was still feeling smugly neutral when he gave his famous victory gesture. The crowd gave a tremendous shout and I heard a loud yell very close to me. I'll tell you just how close—the yell was coming from me. In a detached moment of clarity, I found myself up in the air, waving my arms wildly and shouting. It was like literally being beside myself. When I landed, I quickly used a neutralizing technique that I will teach you shortly, and I was able to regain my neutrality. But it shook me up and forever convinced me of the power of crowds.

Intellectual Telepathy
Intellectual telepathy occurs in the head, and the emotions aren't involved except as your own personal reactions to

whatever the telepathic message is. There are three forms of this kind of telepathy:

Visual. This is an image that pops up in your mind for no apparent reason at all. It can last a few seconds, or it can turn into a spontaneous daydream. Most often people shrug off such images or ignore them completely, unless they happen to be vivid and followed by an event that gives them meaning. As an example, suppose you suddenly got an image of a rose as you woke up in the morning and someone "surprised" you with a rose as a gift in the afternoon. That would be this kind of telepathy in operation. So would the sudden image of a friend whom you found out later was thinking or talking about you at that moment. Note, however, that you may get a sudden image and never know what it was about, because although it is possible to receive a purposely sent telepathic image, it's also possible to pick up stray images not intended for you. How can you tell the difference? Unless you are purposely seeking or expecting an image, you can't. Sorry about that.

Verbal. This happens when you clearly hear a voice, but there's no one nearby speaking. Sometimes you can hear a person in the next room calling your name, but when you go there you find that they didn't. Usually the person will admit thinking about you and perhaps wishing you were there to share something. The thought may have been vague and not intended as telepathy, but you received it as a definite call. Telepathy will often take the form of clear words or phrases, with or without meaning. Again, you may never know why you heard it. The other morning I was awakened by the soft voice of a man saying, "Please." I still have no idea who it was or why he said it. The message, if it was a message, may not even have been meant for me. Sometimes we can overhear conversations in the subjective world just like we do in the objective world.

Another way that verbal telepathy shows itself is when you say the same thing at the same time as someone else. As a teenager, I had a close friend with whom this sort of telepathy would occasionally occur. Generally we got a lot of laughs from it. There was one time, though, when it was no longer funny. As we were riding in a car, we started to speak, said the same thing, laughed, and tried again. It happened a second time, then a third and a fourth. By then we were upset with each other, so we remained silent for about ten minutes while both of us wildly thought of something so outlandish to say that the other couldn't possibly think of it. Suddenly we turned to each other in the same moment and said exactly the same outlandish thing to each other! It took another half hour of silence for this exceptional rapport to run its course.

Auditory, Olfactory, etc. Sometimes we clearly receive sounds, smells, senses of being touched, and other sensory inputs that do not have an objective-world source. These can happen at any time, and on occasion they may wake us up because they seem to be coming from outside of us.

The actual source may be hard to identify, because sometimes the sound of a loud knocking on a door may relate to a need in your outer environment, like the time my cat wanted to be let out in the middle of the night, and sometimes the same sound may wake you up to find nothing you can relate to at all. Not long ago my wife and I both heard the sound of soft chimes just as we were about to go to sleep, and there was nothing in our environment that could account for it, nor has anything related to chimes turned up in our daily life. Telepathic sounds *may* have meaning, but they do not *necessarily* have meaning.

Ideatic. Here is telepathy without words or images, just ideas. The sudden urge to call someone or do something is frequently the result of this kind of telepathy. Scientists who make the same discoveries, inventors who invent the same inventions, and writers who come up with the same storylines are experiencing this kind of telepathy, too. I have experienced this kind of telepathy when writing a novel and a character I never thought of suddenly appears in my mind with a full history and "insists" on being included.

All forms of intellectual telepathy break into your awareness most easily during the moments just after waking up and just before falling asleep. Try to pay more attention to what is going on in your mind at those times, and you may be astonished at how much telepathy you are receiving.

Active Telepathic Receiving

Now we can have more fun because we are dealing with the conscious development of telepathic receiving ability. There are three forms to consider: scanning, tuning, and resonating.

Scanning

Scanning is like moving the dial of a radio or television from station to station or channel to channel just to see what's on the air. Your purpose in doing so will be to see what kind of telepathy you pick up naturally. The choice your body mind presents to you will tell you much about yourself and the kinds of beliefs you hold.

To practice scanning, all you do is take about three extra breaths to prime your receiving set, sit quietly, and pay attention. I suggest you close your eyes as well. Now simply watch every sight, listen to every sound, and feel every sensation that occurs inside your mind or your body. For instance, sounds in your physical environment don't count. Conversation in your head does. Don't try to control anything or force the thoughts into any particular pattern. Allow them to form and develop naturally.

Scanning will give you practice at paying attention to subtle sensations. It is a kind of warming-up exercise for any sort of esper development. Five minutes at a time is enough, because you should write down your experiences in a special notebook for keeping track of your progress.

If you have never let your mind go like this before, two things might happen. Either you could be overwhelmed with images and sounds, or you could draw a complete blank. In the first case, there is nothing to worry about. It is as if you have taken the lid off a pressure cooker and have experienced the first outrush of steam. This phenomenon might continue the first few times you practice scanning, but gradually it will become reasonable. Nevertheless, pay attention to such suddenly released thoughts and feelings and record them in your notebook. They will be full of insights that your body mind has been trying to present to you from various sources.

In the second case, that of drawing a complete blank, there is also nothing to worry about. You have probably just become so good at keeping the lid on the pressure cooker that it won't come off easily. After several scanning sessions, with a serious desire to open up, the lid will come off, and then you will probably be overwhelmed for a while. The release of these backed-up sensations is important, because if you continue to block them you will find yourself blocking other input as well.

Tuning

Tuning is like setting your dial to a particular channel or station; the idea is that we "tune in" to something. In terms of your focus mind, all it really means is "directed attention." In other words, to tune in to something, all you do is direct your attention to it. In order to tune in to another person's thoughts, you simply think of the person and pay attention to the images and other sensations that your body mind gives you.

Does this sound too easy? Well, that's why it's been a secret for so long. Because telepathy is considered to be such a strange thing in our society, people find it difficult to believe that it doesn't take special talents and complicated training. Once you discard that belief, you will find it easy to do.

Tuning in is not hard at all. The hardest parts are relaxing enough so that you can pay attention to what is coming in and to interpreting the results. Relaxation is the real key to enhancing your esper awareness. If you are anxious, worried, or disturbed in any way, your receiving ability will be diminished. It is important to note that when I say *relaxation*, I mean relaxation of your body muscles. It is futile to try to relax your mind without relaxing your body. You may succeed in suppressing your thoughts, but that is not relaxation. When your mind is disturbed, various muscles become tense. This constricts your energy flow and cuts down on your ability to receive subtle impressions by choice. The energy exercise given above will help greatly in relaxing your body.

Interpretation is another matter. This is what actually sets the esper apart from the average person. The esper has learned how to interpret what is received. Unfortunately, I cannot (nor can anyone else) give you a firm set of rules for interpretation. Your body mind talks to you in a language that is uniquely yours, based on your own set of beliefs and experiences. The culture you share with others provides some common ground for interpretation, but overall you'll have to learn your own interior language. One esper may receive an image of a rose and interpret it correctly as love; another esper may receive the same image and interpret it correctly as sadness. The meaning is not in the rose itself, but in what the rose means to the esper. This is why you will want to keep a record of your esper impressions as you practice the exercises. By periodically checking your results, you will eventually build up your own accurate system of interpretation. Here are some exercises to help you develop your tuning ability:

Exercise 1. Sit quietly and think of a person you know. A friend who is on vacation would be a good choice, because you won't be so apt to interfere consciously with your knowledge of the person's habitual routine. Make the contact by constructing a mental image of the person or using a photograph. Then simply let your focus mind observe and record what the body mind tells it. You may get disconnected images, a daydream-like sequence, con-versation, snatches of music, body sensations, or some-thing else. Pay attention to everything and write it all down, including the time. Some people do this better with their eyes closed, others with eyes open. Make your choice. Don't spend more than five minutes at this exercise without reestablishing contact by visualizing the person or looking at the photo. When you are ready to stop, tell your body mind to cut the contact by saying "Stop," "Over and Out," "Finish," or some such thing. Some people find it easier to write down their impressions as they get them, while others prefer to wait until the session is over. As soon as you can, check with the person you focused on to see whether anything they were doing at that time or on that day corresponded with what you received. If nothing seems to correspond, don't be discouraged. It may be just a question of interpretation. Also, you should check the later section on troubleshooting to see whether you might find an answer there.

Exercise 2. You can do this exercise with just one other person—one of you acting as the sender (whom we will assume has studied the appropriate section further on) and one as the receiver. However, you will learn more about the variations in telepathy if you do the exercise with one sender and several receivers. Arrange for the sender to transmit a mental image for a definite period of time, say, two or three minutes at the most. The sender should announce the moment he or she is ready to begin transmitting. At that moment, focus your attention briefly on the sender and then pay attention to every image and sensation your body mind gives you—no matter how silly or irrelevant they may seem—until the exercise is over. Afterward, check your results with the sender and refer to the section on troubleshooting. A complete practice session should include no more than ten transmissions spaced a few minutes apart. Beyond this limit, you may find that your energy level is too low to get good results. Remember that concentration over time may cause the body mind to resist what you are doing and tense up.

Exercise 3. This is an interesting variation on exercise 2. The only difference is that the sender uses a physical picture (as from a book or a magazine) to transmit instead of a mental image. By the way, images are used by the sender because the body mind responds better to them than to words, even though you might receive the interpretation in words.

Resonating

Resonating refers to a technique used by ancient wise men to gain knowledge of a thing. In a way, it is just an extension of tuning in, but carried to the point where you find yourself apparently observing something from within, rather than receiving impressions from a distance. It is closely related to empathy. To understand the nature and function of a plant, for instance, these ancients would "penetrate" the plant with their minds and later record their impressions. This explains to a great extent how the ancients were able to know much of what they did without benefit of modern technology. Again, the actual technique is simple. It is mostly a matter of trusting your impressions. You can do it, too, and the next exercise is designed to show you how.

Resonating Exercise. This exercise can be done by yourself, but it's more fun to do it in a group and compare your experiences. First, select a small houseplant. Sit near it and gaze at it for a while. When you feel ready to begin, close your eyes and imagine yourself moving toward the stem of the plant and growing smaller and smaller until you reach and go right through the stem and into the plant. Imagine yourself in the plant and small enough to move around easily and observe the action of the sap and cells. Travel into the roots for a few moments, then slowly move up the stem into a branch and a leaf. Explore the leaf and exit into the air and back to yourself when you are through. This process should take at least five minutes. Don't rush it. During the whole experience, be as aware of everything as you can—sights, sounds, colors, feelings, etc. For another interesting experience, try a crystal.

I can already hear many of you asking, "But wasn't that just imagination?" Of course it was imagination, but that doesn't mean it wasn't a real experience. Imagination is simply the power of making images in your head. Important things espers do are to treat those images as if they had meaning, to learn to interpret that meaning, and, if they are good, to test their validity (effectiveness). For instance, with the plant exercise above, you could extend your sense of awareness to determine whether the plant had any deficiencies that needed correcting. In your journey through the plant you could feel very thirsty, possibly meaning the plant needs water, or you could just suddenly "know" that it needs more iron. The plant might even seem to talk to you in words. The test for validity comes afterward, when you give the plant iron or water or whatever and see how that changes its growth or appearance. If nothing changes or the plant gets worse, then the first thing you check is your interpretation, not the reality of the experience. If you experienced it, then it must be real. That is a simple fact you might think seriously about. The only thing you can reasonably question is the meaning of the experience. If the plant improves, your interpretation was valid.

Some of you will undoubtedly cry, "Coincidence!" If by that you mean an accidental, nonrelated chance happening, then you are in trouble in terms of becoming an esper.

It is essential for the development of your ESP abilities to accept the idea that your outer and inner experiences are related. Otherwise, you'll never trust your own sensations; you'll be like an unemployed wine taster who has stopped believing in his taste buds. Claiming "coincidence" is a cop-out for the fearful. To titillate your think tank further, I remind you that the idea of coincidence is just another interpretation. But is it valid (effective)?

MENTAL STRUCTURES FOR TELEPATHIC RECEIVING

Among the many techniques for learning telepathic reception, you will often run across the practice of imagining a blank movie screen and letting the telepathic information appear on it. This is what I call an "esper structure," a mental device to make the process easier. I say, if it helps, use it. But a screen doesn't work for everyone, so don't limit your creativity. Personally, I find that a screen really cramps my style. Nowadays I rarely use any kind of structure, but that isn't necessarily a better method. It's just my way. For those of you who might find it helpful, here is a list of ideas for esper structures that you can adapt or change any way you like. Remember, you use your imagination to create the structures:

1. A human or humanoid helper who dashes off and brings you the information in words and pictures (elves and fairies are favorites);
2. Animals who do the same thing (a friend uses a unicorn). This is very popular among shamans;
3. A videophone (more sophisticated than a movie screen); a communications relay satellite; an image of a simple round circle in which the information appears, as text or images.

PHYSICAL STRUCTURES FOR TELEPATHIC RECEIVING

Every culture in the world has developed some sort of physical tool for receiving telepathic information. The process is usually called "divination," unfortunately defined too often as "seeking information about the future or the unknown by supernatural means." All that tells us is that the people who wrote the dictionary don't know anything about it. At least one good dictionary defines it as "having perception by intuition or insight."

I'm about to tell you a huge secret, so pay attention: The only benefit of any of the thousands of divination tools that people have developed through the ages is to help you become better at tuning in to something. Everything else said about them is hype. On the other hand, helping you to tune in to someone or something can be a really, really, good benefit. And just as we use different tools for gaining knowledge in the objective world according to what we want to know (books, magazines, newspapers, websites, etc.), so we can use different tools in the subjective world for gaining the kind of knowledge we want, too.

As I said, there are thousands of kinds of divination tools, but the most well-known today are the tarot cards (and their many modern variations) and the Chinese *I Ching*. I talk about other, less well-known tools in my books *Urban Shaman* and *Earth Energies*. You can find a good variety of these tools at most regular bookstores and any metaphysical store, so I won't bother to describe these systems here. I recommend, however, that you consider using them as tools for training your own tuning ability.

Another tool for tuning in, well-known but greatly misunderstood, is a crystal ball. In my early research, I ran across a description of the seventeenth-century English metaphysician John Donne seeking information from a crystal ball. Great emphasis was put on the need for a perfect crystal and the use of a young virgin boy to do the actual seeing, as well as on the need for a certain amount of ritual. The belief at the time, which still persists, is that an image will appear within the crystal. After years of in-depth research and practice, I discovered that, after gazing at the crystal for a while, your mind creates a sort of screen over the crystal on which images from your mind can appear.

This explains why so many variations of this practice have been developed by cultures around the world. In ancient Egypt, the seers used a clear pool of water. In Mongolia, shamans use a polished disk of brass. In my Hawaiian collection of divination tools, I have a "magic mirror" made of polished basalt that was placed in a stone bowl and covered with water to produce the same effect. And it was during my research that I remembered an almost forgotten experience with my Italian grandmother, who taught me how to divine using a spot of sunlight on a Formica table in her kitchen.

These days, for students who are interested, I recommend either a circle drawn or printed on a white sheet of paper, or a hoop of any material (like those used in embroidery or weaving). A size of four to six inches (ten to fifteen centimeters) seems to work best. Begin by relaxing and breathing deeply or using the energy exercise on page 68. Then just gaze at the space within the circle with a soft focus, with or without an intention. Typical results may be a feeling of increasing energy and maybe even a visual sense of movement within the circle, an effect like a bowl forming in the circle, or an effect like an upside-down bowl forming above it. With practice, there will also be images, like short daydreams. Remember that some people work better with a physical structure, and some people prefer to do without it.

A simplified version of a more unusual physical structure used for telepathic receiving generally goes by the name of a "radionics" or "psychotronic" device. In this book I'll call it a Telepathic Receiving Device (TRD). In my book *Earth Energies*, I describe these devices in detail and give the plans for a simple one; here is a more simplified version:

First, a bit of essential background. A TRD helps you fine-tune your focus (or fine-focus your tuning, whichever you prefer). The fundamental form of such a device consists of an input component, which is just some physical way of expressing the information you are receiving; an amplifier of some kind for increasing the effect; and an output component for telepathic sending. In this section we will only be concerned with the input. If you feel the need for an amplifier, use the breathing exercise on page 68.

In most TRDs the input component is a pendulum or a pad of some kind that you rub your fingers on. Here is a brief description of how each of these works (and don't be bothered by the fact that many people won't agree with this). A pendulum—any object hung on a string or chain that is able to swing freely—works by responding to micro-muscular movements of your fingers, which are themselves responding to a focused question you ask about something. The pad that you rub is similar, except that it isn't making any response. In this case, all the response is coming from your fingers as they rub. In response to your question, they will either slide smoothly or seem to "stick" to some degree. The latter is caused by microchanges in pressure and/or changes in skin friction.

For best results, you want to give your body mind instructions (telepathically or out loud) on how to respond to your questions (telepathic or out loud). The pendulum has the greatest range of responses, because you can choose what meaning to give to the following kinds of responses: clockwise circle, counterclockwise circle, back-and-forth swing, side-to-side swing. You could refine this by giving additional meanings to the amplitude of the swings. The finger-rub is limited to slide and stick, but, with practice and attention, you can develop awareness of differences in degree of slide and stick that can give you additional information.

The types of questions are limited only by your imagination and creativity. The types of answers may seem to be limited to yes and no, or simple choices between two or more things; but, used in the right way, they become an unlimited source of information. Below is a list of some of the possibilities using only yes/positive and no/negative answers, with a stillness response for the pendulum and

87

a semistick for the rub to indicate uncertainty. Some categories work best with a list of choices.

Selection

- Choosing the best foods, vitamins, minerals, medicines, remedies
- Choosing a job, career, employee, school, course, teacher, or area in which to live or take a vacation
- Making choices between any two or more items

Analysis

- Analyzing the content of foods or mineral samples
- Analyzing the condition of the physical body or any object
- Analyzing the structure of complexes and belief systems

Evaluation

- Determining physical, emotional, mental, and spiritual compatibility for people, places, animals, plants, and things
- Evaluating qualities or characteristics of people, places, and things

Measurement

- Measuring anything that can be measured, such as time, space, volume, distance, pressure, depth, range, density, intensity, and frequencies

Indication

- Indicating direction, location and boundaries

Communication

- Communicating with the subconscious or telepathically with anyone or anything

The material or form of the pendulum doesn't really matter, as long as you like it. Some people like them long and some like them short, some like natural materials and some like manufactured ones. I have about a dozen pendulums that I like, but my favorite is a silver keychain/knife/fingernail file/mermaid medallion that I got as a gift when I was in Africa. As for the pad, portable is the most practical, and smoothness is the key. I like to use a flat, polished piece of labradorite that I keep on my desk, but an old plastic credit card or membership card will work just as well. When I don't have anything suitable with me, I just rub my thumb against my first two fingers.

Since the primary assumption of second-level reality is that everything is connected, it stands to reason that what you want to check with the pendulum doesn't have to be right in front of you. At the risk of repeating some of my experiences recorded in *Earth Energies*, I want to mention the possibility of remote dowsing. (Dowsing is a subjective way of gaining information about someone or something with the help of a tool like a rod or a pendulum, and it is used most often as a second-level way of searching for water. Remote dowsing is the same thing done at a distance by using a symbol or representation of the person, place, or thing you want to dowse.)

I first learned how to remote dowse from an old Frenchman in Paris when I was on vacation from my job in Africa. He taught me how to determine a person's physical condition from a photograph using a pendulum. Shortly after, I used it to know if a friend was going to wear a tie to a party and whether another friend in England was going to have a baby boy or girl. My most dramatic experience was when my middle son wandered away from home at the age of seven and I found him by using a pendulum on a map of Los Angeles.

A final caveat for this section: Please don't forget that the answers you receive via these divination structures are coming through the filter of your own body mind, and please remember that the answers may not always be accurate, for any number of reasons (excessive tension, change of circumstances, biased frame of reference, etc.). Always use additional ways of checking for validity if the issue is an important one. It's only information, after all.

SOME WORDS ABOUT THE THIRD EYE

A tremendous amount of silliness has been written about the "third eye," a sort of spiritual center located in the forehead that must be "opened" before esper talents can be activated. And of all the silly things that have been written, the silliest was in a book that came out in the 1970s about a Tibetan monk who supposedly had surgery to cut a slit in his forehead that was held open by pins of some kind so that light could enter and turn on his third eye. Others have written that the pineal gland is located in the brain behind the forehead and that esper abilities will be activated by concentrating on that area during meditation. That's silly, because the physical location of the pineal gland is deep in the center of the brain, almost directly behind the eyebrows.

The first thing to know about the third eye is that it does not have a physical location. Behind all the hype is the simple fact that the third eye is the "eye" of your imagination, and imagination is a vital aspect of all esper abilities.

The second thing to know is that the eye is just a metaphor for all the sensory talents of your imagination. Yes, we often mean the visual aspect when we talk about imagination, but the other sensory aspects are important, too.

The third thing to know is that there is also some valid information within the third eye silliness.

For one thing, right behind your forehead are the frontal lobes of your brain. These two lobes are directly involved in your ability to imagine, and imagination is directly involved in your ability to feel emotions. For this reason, from 1890 well into the 1980s a psychosurgical procedure called a lobotomy was performed on tens of thousands of people, primarily in the United States, as a treatment for mental and emotional disorders ranging from simple moodiness to violent, antisocial behavior. In one famous case, a young girl was lobotomized just because her father didn't like her interest in boys, and as a result the girl suffered severe mental retardation for the rest of her life. Lobotomy consists of penetrating the brain with a surgical instrument and removing sections of the frontal lobes or cutting them up to sever connections with the rest of the brain. This reduces or destroys the imaginative ability, thus reducing or destroying emotional reactions. Since imagination is also related to our creativity and learning ability, mental function in general may be reduced or destroyed. In West Africa the same effect is achieved with herbs to produce zombies, but in the modern, more civilized world it is done with the use of drugs.

For another thing, concentrating your attention on your forehead actually does stimulate your frontal lobes and increases your imaginative faculties, including your faculty of inner vision. So, focusing on your third eye where your third eye would be if you had a physical third eye can improve your esper abilities. The process is simple:

1. Find a quiet place. In a comfortable position, close your eyes, and put your attention on your forehead.

2. As a way of maintaining your attention and increasing the effect, consciously inhale and exhale gently as you keep your attention focused. Five minutes is good enough to start.

3. Note that you may experience strange sensations or none at all. Among the strange sensations may be a sense of tightness in your forehead, tingling that may or may not radiate outward, tension released in other parts of your body, or visions of colors or scenes. If the sensations become too uncomfortable, either rub your fingers across your forehead to relieve them, or just stop.

TROUBLE-SHOOTING FOR TELEPATHIC RECEIVING

Telepathy is a subtle kind of perception that is subject to a lot of interference of various sorts. A lack of understanding of what these interferences are has caused many a laboratory experiment to fail and many a skeptic to be convinced that telepathy is nonsense. In this section I will list the major reasons for receiving failures, some of which I believe are my own discovery, because I have never heard or seen them mentioned anywhere else.

Counter Programs

The term *counter programs* refers to beliefs that telepathy doesn't exist, or that, if it does, you don't have the ability. Needless to say, they work as effective blocks to conscious reception.

CHAPTER 5

Symbolic Reception

Sometimes you receive "directly," that is, with sensations that duplicate the physical world, but at other times you may receive "symbolically." The latter would be like receiving an image of a stretched rubber band to symbolize that someone was under tension. The problems here are of two types:

Noninterpretation. This simply means you don't know what the symbol means. You can't make an association; it doesn't make sense.

Misinterpretation. Here you have just given a different interpretation to the symbol from the one that was intended. For instance, a symbol of a car out of control, meaning a person doesn't feel in control of his or her life, might be misinterpreted as a person physically being in such a car.

Static

Whenever other feelings or thoughts interfere with reception, we call them static, like radio static. The categories are:

Emotional Static. If you are in the throes of emotional difficulties, you won't be able to receive clearly, if at all.

Intellectual Static. This occurs when you are concentrating so strongly on something that no telepathic input can penetrate your consciousness. When I was about fifteen, my father and I were cultivating corn in a field. Thinking my mind would be clear, my father tried to transmit something to me telepathically. When I didn't respond, he questioned my openness to reception. But what he didn't know was that, far from being clear, my mind was intensely occupied with a fantasy adventure that effectively blocked out anything else.

Distortion

In the case of distortion, reception has taken place, but the content of the message has been distorted beyond recognition. We can distinguish two types:

Emotional Distortion. A woman with good news excitedly made telepathic contact with her mother to get the latter to call. The mother got the message, but she distorted the feeling of excitement into one of danger to her daughter and was highly overwrought by the time she called. Emotions can be transmitted, but it is a tricky business.

Symbolic Distortion. An example of symbolic distortion would be someone sending you an image of a crosswalk on Delaware Street in Washington, D.C., with the message to meet them there, and you receiving an image of

Washington crossing the Delaware. Another example would be your spouse sending you a message to pick up a head of lettuce and you coming home with cabbage.

Partiality and Exaggeration

I have found partiality and exaggeration to be quite common when transmitting a picture to a group of people. There is a tendency for the body mind to focus on just a part of the picture being sent and/or to exaggerate it out of proportion to the rest of the picture. In receiving a picture of a country scene with some ducks in a pond in a corner, a person might just get one big image of a duck. And another person might get one of the trees and nothing else. Still others might get a sense of peace with no images. Partiality and exaggeration occur to some extent in all telepathic reception because of unconscious preference, based on experience and memory. These preferences then act as screens or filters through which the message must pass. As a matter of fact, quite a few of the difficulties encountered in telepathic receiving are due to personal preferences that block out a lot of incoming material.

By practicing and keeping records of your experiences, you can find out what your unconscious preferences are and, when and if you want to, you can remove the consequent barriers by self-suggestion.

Bleed-Through

I discovered a curious thing in my classes whenever I was transmitting a picture from a book. Often people would get a clear image that had nothing to do with the picture I was sending. For a while I thought this was avoidance (see below), but then one time I happened to glance at a picture on the back of one I was sending and realized that several people in the class had picked up that picture instead. Since that time, the same thing has happened so often that I know now it is a regular part of telepathy. Not only will people pick up the picture on the reverse page, but some have tuned in to pictures as much as three pages away from the one I was sending. The unanswered question is whether my senses are penetrating the book and transmitting more than I realize or whether their senses are projecting outward to penetrate the book on their own. I suspect the former is the case, but it should make interesting research for someone. Another effect that might be called "bleed-over" is when several pictures are on one page. Although the sender may be concentrating on just one, the receivers will often pick up on what is in the sender's peripheral vision.

Crossover

Crossover happens when you are trying to tune in to one person and your body mind gives you information from another person present. It has to do with those personal preferences I spoke of. It is as if your body mind finds the other person's thoughts more interesting. It happens frequently in a class situation, and some of you who have visited an esper reader with a friend may have found the esper reading for your companion instead of for you.

Delayed Reception

For many possible reasons (preoccupation, tension, emotional upset, etc.), you might not receive telepathic information consciously when it is being sent, but it pops up later on that day or maybe even in your dreams. It is as if your body mind puts the message on hold until your mind is free enough to receive it.

Avoidance

This is a fear syndrome. Even though a person might believe in telepathy and consciously desire to develop it, there may be an underlying fear of it. This usually results in one of three things where receiving is concerned: substitution of an unrelated image by the body mind; no sensations at all; or a tendency to fall asleep while trying to receive. The more the person continues to work with telepathy and realizes that it is a natural human trait, the sooner such fears will be dissipated.

TYPICAL TELEPATHY EXPERIMENTS

To give you an idea of what may happen in a telepathic training session, I will describe the results of three class experiments. The students were all adults, ranging in age from eighteen to over sixty. There were fourteen people, but not everyone received something in each experiment, so I won't list the blanks. None of the people in the group had ever consciously tried to receive before.

Experiment One

I sent a strong mental image of a volcano erupting for one minute. What follows is a list of what the class received:

- A camera (seemingly unrelated, but the image could have triggered an association with tourism or with the shape of the lens)
- A circle (a case of symbolic distortion related to the shape of the crater)
- Two people saw a mountain (partiality)
- A blackboard (I suspect avoidance)
- A pyramid with a rainbow over it (interesting symbolic distortion)
- Something mechanical (could be either avoidance or crossover)
- A bright red orange and an apple (symbolic reception)

- A lamp (symbolic reception)
- A pelican (probably avoidance)
- An orange moon (a combination of partiality, exaggeration, and symbolism)

Experiment Two

I transmitted a mental image of a tropical scene with palm trees, a stream, mountains, and so on. During this class I was wearing a pendant that is symbolic of this Hawaiian-based knowledge as well as a kukui-nut lei. Three people received my pendant (symbolic reception); four people just saw me (curious symbolic reception). Others saw:

- The lei I was wearing (symbolic reception)
- A bird (partiality)
- Telephone wires (possibly a partial and distorted pick-up on the stream, or on the act of telepathy itself)
- Mountains and Hawaii (good direct pick-up)
- A pressure in the head (probably avoidance)
- An animal, a tree, and water (partiality)

Experiment Three

This time I transmitted a picture from a book. The picture was a simple, white, cellular structure. On the same page were an underwater scene and a pattern of layered lines. Note how some body minds added more details to make the material more interesting. Here is what was received:

- A city (possible symbolic distortion due to the block arrangement of the cells)
- Wavy snow and snow on a mountain (symbolic distortion)
- Black and white (partiality)
- Light sky (partiality and symbolic distortion)
- Seashore with a small boat (bleed-over and distortion)
- Layers of rock (symbolic distortion and bleed-over)
- Live "shooting" coral (bleed-over and symbolism)
- Underwater (direct bleed-over)
- Sun with diagonal lines and shadows (distortion and possible bleed-over)
- A tropical ocean (symbolic distortion and bleed-over)

The high rate of bleed-over on this one was no doubt due to the rather uninteresting nature of the picture being sent. None of these students had any training other than an hour's explanation before they started.

THE NEUTRALIZING TECHNIQUE

No, I haven't forgotten. There is more than one way to neutralize the telepathic influence of other people, intentional or not, and they all involve some way to concentrate your focus mind in order to disempower the influence. However, the following method is my favorite because it is so simple and effective. It's called the "One-Inch Belief"— inspired by martial artist Bruce Lee, who developed a fighting technique called the "One-Inch Punch." I'll have more to say about that in a later chapter.

Not too long ago, I was seeking a way to help people get centered quickly when they were emotionally upset or mentally confused. After quite a bit of experimenting, I found that the most efficient solution was to concentrate on a very short statement of something the person believed was true without any doubt. The results were dramatic. With just a few repetitions of the belief, emotional upset and mental confusion gave way in moments to clarity and relaxation.

It was the brevity of the statement that led me to call it the "One-Inch Belief." "I am here," "God loves me," "Water is wet"—all have provided excellent results for different people. Although originally designed for therapy, this technique later proved to work equally well for centering and the neutralizing of unwanted telepathy.

With the above described uses of telepathy—to receive information—reality can change because you change your attitudes and/or behavior due to the new information received. In the next chapter you'll discover methods of more directly influencing change.

Chapter 6

Telepathic Projection

T here cannot be any telepathic receiving unless there is telepathic projection. Everyone is projecting telepathically all the time, but not everyone is necessarily listening. To use a modern analogy, some people are projecting by satellite, some by cable, and some by regular TV. There are some common channels, but others are exclusive to the system. For instance, the nonprofit publishing company that I run, called Hunaworks, produces videos that are presented on a local public cable channel. However, I can't watch them because at home I have a satellite system that doesn't access that cable channel. On the other hand, I get music channels that neither the cable system nor the regular TV system can access, so people using those systems can't hear that music.

The point is that, similarly, telepathic sending will not be received by everyone you may want to reach. That's why massive, worldwide prayer or meditation events for peace have so little effect. They have *some* effect, of course, but you don't see significant numbers of fighting people laying down their arms and hugging each other right after these events. If you're not using the right channel as well as the right system, you're not getting through.

In general, continuing the metaphor, total strangers not in your immediate environment behave like they are on a different system. People you know behave like they are using the same system no matter where they are, although they might not be tuned to the same channel when you are sending, and strangers in your immediate environment act like they are on the same system, but not necessarily on the same channel. There are exceptions for various reasons—this is only a metaphor, after all. However, it's valid often enough for it to be a good general rule.

THE MYTH OF MIND CONTROL

One of the greatest barriers to learning esper skills is the totally false idea that one person can control the mind of another. I have been studying and practicing esper abilities and techniques since the age of fourteen; I have explored the esper methods used in many countries and cultures, including having direct experience with the voodoo masters of West Africa; I have run a professional hypnotherapy clinic for ten years; and I can tell you this unequivocally: no one, anywhere, in any way, no matter what they claim or believe, has the power to control another person's mind. In fact, esper communication is not all that different from face-to-face communication. If you are unethically inclined and know how to do it, it is possible to influence another person telepathically to do what you want by intimidation, threat, or blackmail, but in no case is it possible to control the other person's mind and make them do what you want just because you want it. On the other hand, persuasive skills are just as ethical and effective in esper communication as they are in ordinary communication, and that will be covered in the next section.

HOW TO WIN FRIENDS AND INFLUENCE PEOPLE AS AN ESPER

It is a well-known fact in business circles that the best way to get people to buy your product is to sell them its benefits. This is far, far more effective than trying to get them to buy your product because you are such a wonderful person or company, or by listing all the wonderful features of your product. Some people will translate the features into benefits, of course, but too many will not if you don't go out of your way to do the translating yourself. For instance, as I write this I am in the market for a power saw to cut down guava trees in my forest. One store advertised a gasoline-powered chain saw with a feature that said "33 cubic centimeter engine." Well, that's nice, but what does it mean? I know enough about engines to realize that it has something to do with displacement, but so what?

Where is the benefit to me? I could do the research to find out, but like most buyers I won't bother. I'll just buy a different saw that makes the benefits more clear.

What this means in terms of esper sending is that the more clearly your sending includes a benefit to the receiver, the more likely they are to respond to it in a positive way. As an example, if you want to use ESP to attract a friend or a mate, include information about what makes you so attractive. In the simplest terms, motivation is what moves people.

Next, we'll cover different types of telepathic sending.

BROADCASTING

You'll notice that we have to resort to electronic terms to describe this process, because modern languages don't have specific terms relating to telepathy. *Broadcasting* in this context refers to a type of telepathic sending that goes out to more than one person, like a radio or television broadcast that reaches all the receivers in an area. There are two forms of telepathic broadcasting.

Unintentional Broadcasting

Unintentional broadcasting is the other side of empathetic reception. In other words, it is the projection of moods and feelings as well as of thoughts. The stronger the emotion you're experiencing, the more easily it will be felt by those around you. Hard as you try, you cannot keep your emotions to yourself. In the natural course of things, they are projected outward to friends and strangers alike. People who are totally secure and confident in themselves, or who are experiencing at the same time a different emotion just as powerful as yours, won't be bothered by the one you're projecting. But as regards other people, your fear, insecurity, anxiety, depression, or whatever will tend to stimulate the same feelings in them, and they don't even have to be looking at you.

On the plus side, your more positive emotions have the same effect. Your state of happiness, enthusiasm, or confidence will also be transferred to others, and if your feelings are strong enough, they may even change another person's bad mood to a better one.

At some time or another you have surely been in the company of someone whose mere presence just made you feel good. They were, in all likelihood, involuntarily broadcasting their good feelings to you.

Sometimes we can unintentionally broadcast a kind of "shield" that says "Stay away, I want to be left alone." Unless they have their own reasons for ignoring your broadcast, most people will respond by letting you be. The important point here is that people will react to you according to what you broadcast. Put on whatever kind of face you like, say whatever words you will, their reactions to you will mainly correspond to your unintentional broadcasting.

Intentional Broadcasting

Now we can proceed to the conscious direction of what you already do naturally. Intentional broadcasting is the willful sending out of waves of programmed energy to affect the people around you. By doing this you can create your own kind of "charisma" that can be of tremendous value with your family, on your job, and at any gathering where you wish to make an impression or help someone who needs a lift. The simple fact is that you can choose the state of mind that you wish to project.

The important thing is to be able to build up inside yourself the kind of emotion or feeling you want to send out. The breathing exercises from the last chapter will start you off with the basic increase of energy, but you will have to add to that a powerful emotional charge. Quite a few experiments have shown that the easiest positive emotion to generate "on the spot" is enthusiasm. You do that by thinking strongly about what you are try-ing to accomplish, letting yourself get excited about it, and giving yourself a rousing inner pep talk to get the juices going. At this point, you use your imagination to impose a pattern on the energy you've built up. All you do is create a mental image of the condition or state you want to send out and desire it to be sent. The body mind does the rest. The mental image acts like a plan for the body mind to follow, and the desire is like an order that says, "Okay, body mind, this is what I want you to do, so go out and do it!" In fact, using words to keep your own intention and energy focused is an excellent idea. Note that the words themselves are mainly for your benefit. The receiver is unlikely to "hear" specific words. He or she or it will be much more influenced by your energy and intention.

Remember that your body mind is responsible not only for receiving sensory information, but also for sending it out. You don't have to worry, it knows how to do its job. All it needs from you are clear and simple directions. Imagination provides the plan and desire gives the order.

The basic steps for voluntary broadcasting are these:

1. Energize (use deep breathing and build up positive emotion).
2. Visualize (picture the successful outcome).
3. Project (send out) the energized idea. Remember that the idea is projected by desiring it to go forth and by imagining it happening.

BEAMING

Beaming refers to telepathic projection directed toward a single person or well-defined group of persons—or parts of persons, and even things. If broadcasting is like the waves that go out in all directions from a radio or TV transmitter, then beaming is like communication by a laser beam or a cell phone conversation between two people. The two types of beaming are unintentional and intentional.

Unintentional Beaming

Unintentional beaming takes place whenever you think of someone else, and the more emotion involved, the greater the effect. Unfortunately, the result is that any thoughts of hate or anger that you feel toward a particular person are not kept inside your skull. These thoughts go directly out to the person in question and may or may not cause unpleasant effects. A self-confident or well-focused individual will receive little or no effect; others may react with pain or illness. I know there are some people who might say, "Good, it serves them right!" However, you cannot send out any kind of thought without affecting your own system. That means that someone who continually directs vivid and hateful thoughts toward others is committing slow suicide. Even putting aside the moral factor, simple self-preservation has to be given serious consideration. Happily, we cause beneficial effects every time we direct a thought of love, encouragement, or compassion to someone. We are affected, too, and the benefits reflect on us. It is extremely rare for a truly loving person to get seriously ill.

Unintentional beaming is also involved in more neutral events such as when you receive a call or a letter from someone you have been thinking about. Consciously you may not have been aware of much emotion, but a strong inner desire provided the energy to bring the response.

Intentional Beaming

If you have ever stared at the back of a person's neck for the purpose of trying to make them turn around, you have been engaging in intentional telepathic beaming. If you've ever strongly desired a particular person to do a certain thing, you've also been practicing intentional beaming. As you know by now, the difference between broadcasting and beaming is that with the latter you are narrowing your focus to one person (or a limited group of two or three). Other than that, the procedure is much the same except that instead of visualizing a general condition, you focus on an image of the person in the state of doing the thing that you desire.

Intentional beaming is used by millions of people who never give a thought to the assumptions behind what they are doing. Telepathic messages of encouragement sent to distant athletes using a television screen as a point of focus comprise a very popular form of intentional beaming, as do directions given to a golf ball to land in a cup, or dice to land the way you want them to, or any strong wish for someone or something to do what you desire. People know it doesn't always work, for reasons already discussed, but people still keep on doing it because sometimes it does work, also for reasons already discussed.

In a more neutral vein, voluntary beaming comes in very handy when you want to call or contact someone. In the first chapter I mentioned the use of telepathy for calling kids to dinner. This used to be such a natural thing around my house when the kids were still living with us that when my wife asked me to call them she actually expected me to sit down at the table and close my eyes. What I did then was to think of the kids in a loving way and at the same time send a full sensory image of a delicious dinner. Invariably, as long as they were in the neighborhood, they would be home within five minutes, even when they were in separate locations. And just as invariably, they would always say that they just felt like coming home at that time. Never did they say that they "got my message."

There are several important insights we can gain from that experience. First is the fact that the way to tune into someone is simply to think of that person. That's all. Consider it the telepathic equivalent of dialing someone's cell phone. Next, you include a feeling of why you like them if you know them, or mentally give them a compliment of some kind if you don't know them well. This is what gets their subconscious attention. The better you know someone the more practically simultaneous these first two steps are. Then you toss out the prize, meaning you send a thought of something the other person will think is a benefit. Finally, and perhaps at the same time, you transmit a suggestion of what you really want. The person on the other end will follow that suggestion or not, depending on a lot of factors. But the more attractive the benefit, the more likely the person is to follow the suggestion.

Doesn't sound much like mind control, does it? At Second Level, using telepathy you have even less possibility of control than you do in face-to-face communication, because in the former you don't have the option of physical force.

GOING WHERE FEW HAVE GONE BEFORE

Now it is time to stretch some minds. So far, we have concentrated on telepathic communication with people. Remember, however, that one of the corollaries of the idea that there are no limits is that everything can be considered as alive, aware, and responsive. Accordingly, effective telepathic sending can be done with nonhuman entities and even nonorganic objects.

The steps we used above will work equally well in this area. Let's review them before we continue:

1. Think of, or direct your attention to, what you want to communicate with.
2. Evoke a loving or friendly feeling, or at least give a compliment of some kind.
3. Send a suggestion or request for what you want.

4. Send a thought of a potential benefit for doing what you want.

The most important thing to understand is that, the more you know about what or whom you want to communicate with, the easier and more effective it will be. This knowledge includes personal experience as well as learned information. The same is true for humans, of course. The better you know a person, and the more knowledge you have about human psychology, the more effective your telepathic sending will be, assuming that you are open enough to attempt it. Come to think of it, this is the most important thing to understand, no matter what level of reality you are dealing with.

Communicating with Animals

There is a great deal of literature about occurrences of telepathic communication with animals, but very rarely are there any clear-cut instructions for doing it. I'll try to provide that for you here.

Pets are easiest, because you are so familiar with them. If you have a pet, you've probably noticed numerous occasions when it seemed to know exactly what you wanted, and when it seemed to be able to communicate to you what it wanted. By using what I'm teaching, you may be able to have more direct and specific telepathic communication.

Other animals may not be as readily responsive as a pet, but you can still get very good results to the degree that you have some knowledge of their normal type of behavior. Here are some examples of my experiences using the instructions given above.

The Frightened Bird
A small bird about the size of a finch flew through the front door of a house, down a hallway, and into a high-ceilinged living room, where it darted around in a panic. As quietly as possible, I entered the room and sat down. I made myself calm and projected calming thoughts of pretty meadows and birds at rest. It took five to ten minutes before the bird settled down, but it still didn't know how to get out. Then I imagined a path made of golden light going out of the room, through the hall, and out the front door into the open. With that went a suggestion that the bird follow the light. Less than a minute later, the bird did exactly that.

The Frustrated Wasp
In an almost identical situation, a big wasp flew into the large single room of a small building with two large plate-glass windows on either side of the door. The wasp couldn't find its way out and was bumping against the window over and over. I went close to the wasp and used the path of golden light again to show the way out. Seconds later, the wasp followed the path exactly, even though the path

wound around an obstructing pedestal, and flew out into the open air. It seemed to me that it felt happy, but that might be just my personal impression.

Calming Barking Dogs

I have used several techniques with success to calm barking dogs. Projecting blue light around the dogs works quite well, though it may take several repetitions to get the best effect. I have used a telepathic form of the Dynamind Technique (see my book *Healing for the Millions*) successfully a number of times. More recently, I've been using knowledge gained from Cesar Millan, famous as a "dog whisperer," who has an amazing rapport with dogs and is able to heal them of many behavioral problems in a seemingly effortless way. In chapter 2 of his book *Cesar's Way* (Harmony Books, 2006), he has this to say (I have moved one sentence):

> [The] truly universal, interspecies language is called energy. It's a language all animals speak without even knowing it, including the human animal. What's more, all animals are actually born knowing this language instinctually. Even human beings are born fluent in this universal tongue, but we tend to forget it because we are trained from childhood to believe that words are the only way to communicate. The irony is, even though we don't think we know the language anymore, we are actually speaking it all the time. Unknowingly, we are broadcasting in this tongue 24–7! Other species of animals can still

understand us, even though we may not have a clue how to understand them. They read us loud and clear, even when we're unaware that we're communicating!

Millan's idea of this communicative energy might be better understood as emotional energy. Millan promotes what he calls a "calm-assertive" state, which projects messages of confidence and leadership that animals understand very well. In my present neighborhood, there are several groups of dogs who bark furiously whenever someone walks in front of their yard. As long as I am able to hold that calm-assertive state and project a thought of myself as a friendly but aloof pack leader, the dogs immediately stop barking and calm down.

These few examples are given only to get you started. Try the ideas out with the animals of your choice.

Talking to the Weather

Someone once asked me, "How do you talk to the wind?" I told them that I usually say, "Hello, wind."

Millan's idea that all animals communicate through energy as a fundamental language can be interpolated to anything alive—when we assume that everything is alive, aware, and responsive. Although this may not conform to our ordinary assumptions, it works.

To influence the weather most effectively, you need to make friends with it. In practical terms, this means that you learn as much as you can about it and have an interested, appreciative feeling about it. Then you send your suggestion and expect the best.

This technique isn't control, remember. Whenever it can, the weather will cooperate with your suggestion. Temperatures can go up or down, wind can blow or be calm, rain can come or go away, clouds can move where you want them to, hurricanes and tornadoes can change direction, and on and on. It won't always work when you want it to, because sometimes weather has its own agenda, but it will work often enough to convince you that it isn't just coincidence.

As an example, I work with weather often and we have a nice, friendly "relationship," so it cooperates with me more often than not. I always tune in first to receive any impressions that it isn't willing to change, and if I feel that a possibility for change exists, then I put out my suggestions. Just recently, here in Hawaii, we've had a period of drought. Since our soil is so porous, this can mean no rain for five days. In the time I'm speaking of (June 2007), we had almost two weeks of clear, dry weather. Many of us in our area are dependent on rain catchment for all our water, and some families were forced to buy water from commercial sources for their everyday needs. That's when I decided to do something. Even though the forecast was for a week of more dry weather, I spoke to the rain and the wind and asked for help. The next day we had a light drizzle, and the day after we had some nice periods of fairly heavy rain.

Another example of communicating with weather involves my organization, Aloha International, which used to have an annual festival on Kauai in November, one of the heavy rain months. During twenty years of festivals, which included a lot of outdoor activities, we had to move indoors only twice because of rain.

And one final example. During some of the courses we gave on Kauai, we would take a class to the top of the island for a view of the famous Kalalau Lookout, a stunning panorama of emerald green, curtain-like mountains descending to an azure blue sea. As long as the valley wasn't socked in with clouds, that is. This happened frequently, to the great disappointment of large numbers of tourists. However, when we brought a class up and the valley was invisible because of clouds, we would have the class communicate telepathically with the clouds, sometimes accompanied by a chant, and the clouds would *always* part. Most of the time they would completely clear up. Once in a while we would get only a window view, but the clouds always parted for us.

The only thing I have to say further about weather work is, "Try it out."

Telepathic Communication with Objects

Remember that we are working with the subjective worldview here, which says that we can communicate—back and forth—with anything at all. If you are trying to understand this section from an objective worldview, it will not make any sense, because in that worldview objects obviously cannot speak. It is only when we allow ourselves to accept, even temporarily, the subjective-worldview assumptions that we can have a conversation with objects around us.

Actually, many people frequently slip into a subjective worldview without quite realizing that this is what they are doing. In addition to talking to animals and plants as if they had human understanding, a lot of people talk to baseballs, golf balls, and footballs; vehicles and engines; computers and office equipment; and other things. Some of that conversation is encouraging ("Come on, you can do it, keep going!") and some of it is critical ("You blankety-blank good for nothing piece of blank!").

Through years of trial-and-error experimenting, I have found that objects respond much better to encouragement and praise, and the positive effects have gone far, far, beyond any possibility of coincidence. Here are just a few experiences out of literally thousands.

The Happy Bus
Some years back, I participated as a teacher in a shamanic conference in the Yucatan Peninsula of Mexico. Part of what we did was to go to various Mayan sites to do rituals. On one occasion, about twenty or thirty of us took a chartered bus to Uxmal in the northern part of the peninsula, and after a full day we headed south back to Playa del Carmen, around a couple of hundred miles away.

After twenty-five miles or so, we began to hear a loud bumping sound, and the bus started a regular sequence of shaking. The driver stopped the bus and we all got out to see that an inner tube (remember those?) was bulging out of a split in the sidewall of one of the tires. There was no spare, and there were no towns around, so the driver made us all get back into the bus and then drove very slowly southward. Some people from New York wondered why we just didn't use our cell phones to call a repair truck from a local garage. Those of us more familiar with this part of Mexico had to explain that no one had any numbers for whatever phones might be in calling distance, and that there were no local garages and no repair trucks.

After a while someone reminded us that we were a group of people with esper abilities, so why didn't we try to repair the tire with the power of thought? Others suggested we give energy and encouragement to the bus so that it could repair itself. After more discussion, we finally ended up singing love songs to the bus. This went on for a long time until it was completely dark outside, and we were all feeling so high we almost forgot about the tire and our growing hunger. Then, *bam*! The inner tube blew out and the bus rolled to a bumpy stop. The first reaction from everyone was a big let-down that our love songs hadn't worked. Then we looked outside. The bus had stopped right next to the only garage on the highway, and beside the garage was the only restaurant, serving pizza. The inner tube had to blow; we couldn't do anything about that. But from a second-level point of view, the bus was so moved by our love songs that it struggled on until the tube could blow out in the most convenient place possible.

The Cooperative Fan

My second hypnotherapy clinic in Santa Monica, California, was in a shared office space on the second floor of an older building. In the center of the ceiling was a very old recessed fan that ran all the time to bring in fresh air from outside. Unfortunately, it also had a recurring squeak that was distracting and quickly grew irritating. So, one day after work when I was alone in the office, I took the time to thank the fan for doing its job and asked it to stop squeaking. Then I sent it a gift of loving energy. It stopped squeaking immediately and never squeaked again as long as we had our office there. The next morning the other office workers noticed that the fan wasn't squeaking anymore and wondered who had fixed it. I decided that the situation wasn't appropriate to introduce them to the subjective worldview.

Opening and Lifting

One of the most useful applications of the subjective worldview is in the apparently unimportant area of opening things and lifting things. Believe me, there are times when this can be very important. There are a number of ways to make such actions easier, but I like the one that involves compliments and requests. For instance, quite often my wife will ask me to open a jar with a tight lid, and I do it seemingly without effort. At first she was astonished, then later irritated that I could do it and she couldn't, then astonished and delighted again when I showed her how. Usually, though, she still has me do it, because if I'm around it's the "man's job." The process is ultra-simple. When she hands me a jar with a tight lid, I hold it with respect, praise something about it, and ask it kindly to loosen the lid for me. That's it. It works every time, unless I'm too stressed. It works equally well for opening strongly sealed boxes.

For lifting, use the same process. Try it on something reasonably heavy, like a chair or a rock, for a test. Suppose you've chosen a chair. Simply do this:

1. Lift the chair in the ordinary way. Set it down.
2. Compliment the chair for something, like its comfort or its color, and thank it for being available for sitting.
3. Ask it nicely to become lighter so you can lift it easily.
4. Lift . . . and feel the difference.

Chapter 7

Putting Your Aura to Work

~

I n 1975 I was asked to set up a demonstration table for a kind of "esper fair" in the mall of a North Hollywood shopping center. Among other things, I had a device called an "auraboard" (later I'll tell you how to make one) designed to allow people actually to see the aura, or energy field, that surrounds the body. Most people in the mall were ordinary shoppers who stopped by the table out of curiosity.

Every one of the more than a hundred passers-by who tried it was able to see the aura around their hands in thirty seconds or less. The most poignant moment came when I noticed a young woman who had been standing next to the table while about a dozen people tried out the auraboard. When I looked at her she said to me in a very sad voice, "You know, I was put in a mental institution for three years because I could see what all those people are seeing."

That is just one of the unhappy results of ignorance and fear in a society that represses what it cannot understand. There is an energy field around the body that can easily be seen, as you will be able to demonstrate shortly for your-self. But because our school textbooks don't say anything about it and we are generally taught not to trust our own perceptions, even professional psychologists and psychia-trists can make grave errors in determining whether a per-son is suffering from "mental aberrations."

Many practicing espers can tell similar stories of being able to see auras around people when they were young and then discovering to their surprise that not everyone could see them—and further that auras "shouldn't" be seen or you could get in trouble. Most people who find out early that they have this ability either suppress it and forget it to conform with their environment, or just stop talking about it. And yet, the talent is so natural that it can be stimulated in a few seconds with anyone!

SENSING THE AURA

Webster's New World Dictionary defines an aura as (1) an invisible emanation and (2) a particular atmosphere or quality that seems to rise from and surround a person or thing. In popular speech we take the existence of the aura for granted. How often have you heard someone say, "Gee, so-and-so really radiates a good feeling," or "That person certainly has an aura of confidence about him"? Perhaps without consciously realizing it, we are reacting to the person's energy field, and the words we use tell the truth. Of course, telepathy plays a role here, but if it were just telepathy, it wouldn't matter how close we were to the person. Yet the fact is that some people are downright uncomfortable to stand next to, and others make us feel better the closer we are to them (I am including physical contact here). These feelings arise from our contact with the person's "invisible emanation," the aura.

A common question is, "Supposing there is an aura, how far out does it extend?" Well, as far as anyone knows, it extends just as far as gravity or light would. As with those forms of energy, however, a more useful question would be, "How far out is its effective range?" This depends on the individual and on that individual's current state of mental and physical health and focus. Some people radiate a lot of energy naturally and some radiate less. Later you'll learn how to increase your radiation, but for now just think of some parties you've been to. There will usually be a few people who will "stand out in the crowd," not necessarily because of what they wear or how they act or what they look like, but because your eye naturally gravitates toward them. What attracts you, at least in part, is their radiation.

Many entertainers, some athletes, and a few politicians have tremendous auras compared to the rest of the population, and this has something to do with what we call their "charisma." On the other hand, you have undoubtedly run across people whose existence is hardly noticeable. These are feeble radiators. The important thing to know is that, while there are those who are more or less born with a natural ability to radiate great amounts of energy, everyone can be taught how to radiate much more than they do. In other words, *you too can have an aura that people will notice!*

THE AURA IN HISTORY

A long time ago in many parts of the world, it seems that people didn't have as many hang-ups as we do about seeing the aura. They were able to notice how some people radiated much more energy than others, and they began to depict this fact in their art. It became an artistic technique to include an aura around gods, saints, holy men, and heroes whenever artists wanted to show their subjects' extraordinary powers. Today we are left with the remnants of this practice in the silly golden circle that you sometimes see hanging above the heads of cartoon characters. We call it a halo, but it is the same thing as an aura. In the oldest form, it was shown as a circular background for the head. In rare instances the aura around the whole body was shown—the way it actually appears when you learn to see it. It was only when culture caused the suppression of this vision that the artists who didn't understand what it was started drawing it as a suspended ring above the head.

In case you are interested in checking this out, I'll give you a few examples of art from around the world in which the artists have shown the aura in almost exactly the same form. These examples and many others can be found in the

New Larousse Encyclopedia of Mythology (Felix Guirand, ed., The Hamlyn Publishing Group, Ltd., 1972):

- *Christian.* A fifth-century mosaic in the Baptistry of the Orthodox, Ravenna, Italy. The aura is around Jesus and John the Baptist.
- *Ancient Rome.* An undated mosaic of Neptune and his subjects, now in the Louvre Museum. The aura is around Neptune, his consort, Amphitrite, and partially around a cherub-like being who might be Eros.
- *Taoism.* An undated scroll painting depicting Lao Tse.
- *Chinese Buddhism.* A seventeenth-century scroll painting showing five Buddhas, all with auras.
- *Hinduism.* A stone sculpture from the eighth century of Indrani, the wife of lndra.
- *Indian Buddhism.* A second-century stone carving of Buddha sitting under the Bodhi tree.

The fact that the same thing was shown in such widely varying times, places, and cultures suggests that it was a common, shared experience. Or can it be labeled artistic imagination? Let's look at some more modern experiences.

THE AURA AND SCIENCE

The earliest scientific evidence for the existence of the aura in the twentieth century was demonstrated in 1908 by a London medical doctor, Walter J. Kilner. He devised a type of screen filled with a special dye through which a person could look and see someone else's aura. Supposedly, the dye acted to sensitize a person's eyes to higher frequencies of radiation. At any rate, Kilner successfully used the process for medical diagnosis, determining the state of a person's health from the nature of their aura. By the 1920s a number of reputable medical men had endorsed his findings, but Kilner's discovery was too radical for the majority and it died a professional death.

While Kilner's work was receiving professional attention and rejection, Harold S. Burr, PhD., E. K. Hunt Professor Emeritus of Anatomy at Yale University School of Medicine, and his colleagues were researching a curious phenomenon that later came to be called an "L-field." This was an electrodynamic energy field around plants, animals, and people that Burr was able to measure with a sensitive voltmeter. Significantly, the measurements were made without the necessity of physical contact, thus showing that it was indeed a field of energy that was being measured. By 1935 Burr had published a paper called "The Electro-Dynamic Theory of Life." Like Kilner, he found that this field could be used for medical diagnosis, because it changed in intensity and activity according to a person's state of health. More importantly, changes in the field could be detected before a person actually became sick. In spite of more than thirty years of research and published results, however, Burr's work has yet to be accepted by the scientific community.

About the same time that Burr was really getting into his thing—1939, to be exact—a Russian by the name of Kirlian tried to photograph an electric spark and made a discovery that is still shaking up biologists and physicists alike. I suppose by now nearly everyone has heard of Kirlian photography, but in case you haven't, here is a brief review.

What Kirlian did was to develop a technique for photographing what appears to be an energy field around living and nonliving things. Around living objects, the field is a beautifully sparkling, colorful, ever-changing pattern. A fresh leaf has a magnificent pattern, but as the leaf dies so does the field of energy fade away. It can hardly be coincidence that the "Kirlian aura" changes in definite ways according to a person's state of health. So human auras, too, can be used to note illness in the energy "body" before it appears in the physical. After twenty-five years, the Soviet Union finally began serious funding of this kind of research. The research has been known in the United States only since 1970, so in spite of a lot of good independent research replicating Kirlian's results, most Western scientists still scoff at the notion of Kirlian auras.

Nevertheless, the scientific evidence for an energy field around the human body is there, even though it hasn't been fully accepted. It is time to see what the espers have to say about it.

WHAT DO THE ESPERS SEE?

There are many kinds of experience associated with seeing the aura, probably because there are many different kinds of people seeing it. I am going to organize these experiences in terms of stages, but please realize that the development of aura vision does not always progress in a nice, neat, orderly fashion.

Stage One—The Nimbus

The nimbus is what artists draw around the heads of gods and saints, and it is most likely the first thing you will see as soon as you learn how to look for it.

For most beginners, it has the appearance of a hazy light extending a couple of inches out from the head, separated from the head by a thin dark line. I mention the head because that part of the body seems to generate the strongest field. The nimbus can be seen around the rest of the body, but not as easily. The extent and brightness of the nimbus are affected by conditions of health, states of mind, and what we can call the energy reserve. Hence, it is easier to see it around some people than others.

Development of aura vision at this stage involves seeing increasingly more of the nimbus and distinguishing differences in brightness. It is possible you may see the nimbus in a particular color, but at this stage, that has practically no significance. Trying to attach a meaning to color here would be like trying to judge a wine by color alone without ever having tasted any.

Stage Two—Cold Flame

Actually, the flame isn't "cold." It just doesn't have any particular heat, although it resembles heat waves to a great extent. Cold flame is usually seen in the dark or semidark when your senses are wide open. In the beginning, it is easier to see it around yourself, but with practice you can see it around other people and objects as well. In addition to seeing it around an object or person, you may also see it streaming off the fingertips and the top of the head and from the end or corner of an object. Cold flame's appearance is generally blue-gray, but gold and reddish-yellow are not uncommon. Again, color at this stage is not very important. The most striking thing about cold flame is its movement, which usually takes the form of "trembling" and rising.

Stage Three—Flashes and Streamers

Phenomena appearing like flashes and/or streamers of light might be seen coming from any part of the body. The flashes come and go quickly, so it's easy to wonder if you really saw them. The streamers may be either moving or fairly static. If moving, they are like a beam of light that shoots off and disappears. In fact, it is likely that the flashes are moving streamers that we see head-on. Static streamers are most frequently seen emerging from the fingertips, but they can appear elsewhere. Sometimes two broad streamers can be seen emerging from the shoulder blades. This leads to speculation that people in the distant past might have seen these and mistaken them for wings.

Stage Four—Full Surround

Stage four is simply the one at which the nimbus or cold flame is seen surrounding the whole body. For the most part, it looks somewhat like an oval-shaped cloud. It can extend to any distance the esper is able to see, but often it is seen as most dense to a distance equal to a full arm span. By the time this stage of aura vision is reached, it is common for the seer to be able to notice dark patches here and there, which may correspond to areas of present or pending illness.

Stage Five—Rainbow

Now we can talk about color. Espers have a field day telling you how much of what colors you have in your aura and whether you have any missing and so forth. Perceptions vary in regard to color in the aura. Some people see the colors in horizontal layers, others in layers from the outside in, and still others as floating masses of color that interweave and mix.

Interpreting the colors depends on your personal experience. You will perceive the way you believe. Generally, the cool colors denote calm and peace, while the warm colors have to do with activity and excitement. Muddy, washed-out, or unpleasant colors are associated with energy imbalance, negative thinking, and disease. Any other interpretations depend on what the colors mean to the esper. Any esper who cannot see the full spectrum of colors in your aura is giving you an interpretation based on direct telepathy more than anything else (and it could still be very accurate).

Stage Six—Living Light

At this stage, the seer sees not only colors but also shapes that constantly shift and change according to the thoughts and emotions of the individual. Anger has been described as looking like dark red spikes, jealousy like yellow-green hooks, and love like blooming flowers. Of course, there is a lot of personal interpretation involved.

Stage Seven—Fireworks

Imagine an old-fashioned fireworks display surrounding a single person and you can get an idea of what stage seven looks like. Sparklers, whirligigs, bursting rockets, fountains—you name it and it is there. Individual differences show up according to how elaborate and fantastic the display is. Naturally, few people ever experience this stage.

HOW TO SEE THE AURA WITH AN AURABOARD

To start, I have to teach you how to make an auraboard. Now, pay attention because this can get pretty tricky:

1. Find a board.
2. Cover it with adhesive-backed black or white flocking (felt or any other matte material).

Got that? For a board you can use plywood, Masonite, plastic, glass, or anything flat and convenient. As for size, it depends on how you want to use it. For just viewing the aura of the hand, I find that 8 in. × 8 in. (20 cm × 20 cm) is a good size. For classes where I demonstrate the aura around the head and shoulders, I use a board 2 ft. × 4 ft. that I prop on a chair. I have also used a blank flip chart and a white movie screen to good effect.

The purpose of the black or white material is to provide a contrasting background against which the aura can be seen. In my experience, most people are able to see it well against a background of black, but some people do better with a white or light background. As you may guess, an aura-board isn't even really necessary. All you need is any dull, flat surface that you can use as a background. A wall, a brief-case, a desktop, a jacket—anything will work as long as it is of a single color, either very dark or very light, and not shiny.

Watch out for shadows. Arrange the lighting so that you can't see any shadows on the background if possible, because they can interfere with the viewing.

Here we go, you're about to see your aura! What I'll do is instruct you in the same way that I would if we were stand-ing next to each other. I'm assuming you already have your background picked and ready:

Hold one of your hands about five or six inches away from the background with your palm down and your fin-gers spread. Look between the fingers and around the tips of them. What you're looking for is a hazy kind of light. It may be blue-grey or golden or some other color, but it's almost like fog. If you have any trouble seeing it, look right next to the finger, and you should see a dark line. Now look between the dark lines of two fingers and there is the haze. You'll also be able to see the difference between the area between your fingers and the rest of the background beyond your hand.

Do you see it now? If you don't, just relax. It may take a few moments more. A couple of deep breaths will help your ability to see it.

Okay? One more thing. Stare at your hand now for about ten seconds. Keep your eyes fixed in the same spot and take your hand away quickly. See that bright after-image? That's the energy effect that your aura has on your eyes. Now you are a full-fledged aura seer. All you need is practice and you'll be able to see more and more of it with greater ease.

AN OPTICAL ILLUSION?

After I've shown people how to see the aura, someone (maybe you) is bound to ask whether what they've seen wasn't simply an optical illusion. Well, the eyes can be fooled in many ways, and it's a good question. But if it were just an optical illusion, it wouldn't matter whose hand you looked at. The illusion should still be the same. However, the fact is that the aura around the hands of some people will be extremely difficult, if not impossible, to see, while around others it will stand out bright and clear. The after-image, too, will differ greatly in brightness according to whose hand you look at. An after-image is the result of radiant energy impinging on your eyeball. The more energy something radiates, the stronger will be the after-image. These facts argue well against the possibility of optical illusion. So does the fact that you can increase the brightness and radius of your aura at will.

HOW TO INCREASE YOUR AURA

It is quite impressive to put someone against the proper background, have a group of people look at his or her aura, and then tell the person to increase it. The reaction of the viewers is great. And it is so easy to do. Three or four slow, deep breaths will do it automatically.

If you imagine your aura expanding at the same time as you breathe, it will increase even more. And if you imagine a ball of light sitting on top of your head and filling you with energy while you do the previous two actions, you'll be a sure-fire hit. That's all there is to it.

Try it yourself. Once you can see the aura around your hand, practice the above three techniques and note the difference in your aura before and after.

The advantages of increasing the intensity and extent of your aura are several, besides impressing an aura class. This practice alone will help improve your health, attract the attention of other people, help your self-confidence, and help lift you out of negative moods. Just for kicks, try it the next time you are out with friends, at a party or meeting, or need a waiter. If you do it right, you should notice a big difference in the way you are treated. (Don't expect immediate superstar treatment, though. That comes only with a great deal of practice).

OTHER TECHNIQUES FOR SEEING THE AURA

Here are other ways to develop your aura-seeing ability that may take anywhere from a few minutes to weeks of practice:

The Mirror Method

For this exercise, stand in front of a mirror and gaze at a spot about two inches above your head. Keep your focus there, but be aware of your peripheral (side) vision, too. By the way, this works best if either the room behind you is fairly dark or the opposite wall has nothing on it to distract you. Soon you should be able to see the hazy light mentioned above around your head and possibly your shoulders. The dark line right next to your body will be there also. Normally, this ought to take no more than one or two minutes, but if you still don't see anything after ten minutes, stop for the day and try again tomorrow.

The Lightbulb Method

You will need a partner for this technique because it is the partner's aura you will be looking at. First you need a bare lightbulb (lit). Then you stand your partner in front of it so that the bulb is directly behind his or her head. Now you look at your partner's head the same way you would your own if you were using the mirror method. The light shining through your partner's energy field will give a halo effect that should be pretty easy to see. If there were no energy field, there would be no halo, because then your partner's head would simply be sharply outlined against the background.

The Shadow Method

Here is an indirect technique that you may already have witnessed without paying any attention to it. Wait for a bright, sunny day and find a light background, like a sidewalk or a wall. Look at your shadow and bring a hand near your head. Before your hand touches your head, a shadow will appear between them. This shadow is caused by the increased density of your hand's field and your head's field as they blend together. Another way to use the shadow method is to shine a high-intensity lamp on a piece of white paper and bring the shadows of two fingers together slowly. Bright light usually cancels out the ability to see the aura directly (unless your ability is very well developed), but in this case, you will definitely see it indirectly. When your fingers are a quarter to an eighth of an inch apart, a faint shadow will appear between them. This is the shadow of your intensified aura. It may take a few minutes to see it. With practice you will be able to see it when the fingers are a whole inch apart.

The Meditation Method

The name "Meditation Method" refers to the fact that this kind of aura-seeing is often a spontaneous happening during the meditative state. This technique will allow you to see the cold-flame type of aura, but it may take a good deal of practice. Be relaxed yet alert. Seat yourself comfortably in a darkened room (it doesn't have to be pitch black) and focus your eyes in the air about a foot or two in front of you. Don't strain. Just relax and look. Eventually, you will begin to see what looks like bluish "heat-waves" all around you. Twenty minutes at a time is enough to start with until you see it. Often it helps to do this while in an area commonly called a "power spot." One of the strongest heat-wave manifestations I ever experienced was in an area near Kilauea Volcano on the Big Island of Hawaii. If you have time and an absolutely dark room, you can try relaxing and looking for two or three hours at a stretch and see what happens.

THEORY VERSUS APPLICATION

It would be easy to fill many more pages with people's theories of what exactly the aura is, besides just being an energy field. But then all you would have would be a lot of opinions, including mine, and it wouldn't change your ability to see auras or to use them. Theories range from thermal or electromagnetic radiation to complex systems of interwoven energy "bodies" of varying size and densities. All I want to do here is show that the aura does exist and that you can use it, regardless of what you think it is.

Bringing together my various hints and statements, here are some practical uses for the ability to see the aura: as a biofeedback tool for checking your state of health and mind and doing something about it; to increase your all-around sensitivity to your subtle senses; to improve your effect on other people (by intensifying your aura); to check out other people's energy levels (remember, at the beginning, the only valid feedback is brightness and diameter); and eventually, with much practice, to be able to help people by noting areas of energy blockage and pending or current disease.

THOUGHTFORM PROJECTION

A "thoughtform," which I also call a "t-field," is an imagined, energized, 3-D image of a thing or scene that you project with your intent and desire into the world around you. It falls into the category of this chapter because it is really just a condensed portion of your aura.

Thoughtform projection is a concept with which most people are already familiar, but without using the terms I just mentioned. One of the best examples is miming. Marcel Marceau was a master of this art on stage, as Charlie Chaplin was in film. The aspect of miming that interests us most here is that of producing the "illusion" of actual objects so well that the audience suspends disbelief and accepts them as actually being there. Classic examples are a mime washing windows or picking a flower and putting it in his lapel. In theatrical play rehearsals and avant-garde productions, most of the props may be thoughtforms. One of the best modern examples, in my opinion, occurred in the making of *Jurassic Park* where the two children were being chased by dinosaurs in the kitchen. In case you didn't know, during the actual filming the children were required to react to imaginary dinosaurs of their own creation, which they did very convincingly.

The reason I put the word *illusion* in quotes above was to emphasize the fact that, from a second-level perspective, the projected images have a subtle, but tangible, electromagnetic reality. While attention is usually drawn to how well the audience accepts what isn't really there, I want to draw attention to what the human projector is actually doing.

To create the proper effect, the person miming has to externalize an image so intensely, with all the necessary sensory attributes, that his or her body will accept it as real; and, given the right circumstances, anyone else in the area will tend to accept it as real also, at least to some degree. It is my contention that such intensity can actually change the physical environment in ways that can produce mental, emotional, and/or physical reactions in other people. And I don't just mean in an audience. And I don't just mean with people. And I don't mean just while the mime is miming.

Color is a useful tool for thoughtform projection because the body mind reacts extremely well to color transmission. I am speaking here about the visualization of color, the picturing of color in your mind and projecting it out into the world you live in. For many people, it isn't easy to just imagine a color hanging out in space all by itself, and that's pretty abstract for most body minds, anyway. The body mind responds best to an image that has a clear physical basis. Two images that work quite well are a light fog or cloud and a broad-beamed searchlight (with the color filter of your choice). Some people use a whole bank of searchlights for a large crowd.

As for the colors, lots of books will tell you the meanings of various ones according to certain beliefs, but in the final analysis it all depends on how they feel to you. After all, you are the one who will be projecting them, and the visualized colors are really only another way of putting a pattern on the energy you are sending out. Nevertheless, I have found that certain colors give fairly consistent results, so here is a simple and practical list based on experience:

- *Red.* Quite stimulating and attractive, but a little too strong for most purposes because it tends to heighten sexual feelings.
- *Orange.* An energizing color, good for stimulating activity and waking people up.
- *Pink.* Attractive in a friendly way. Promotes cooperation and friendly responses.
- *Green.* Promotes peaceful cooperation and healing of minds and circumstances.
- *Blue.* Very calming. Good for counteracting strong emotions and relieving insomnia.
- *White or Gold.* Promotes feelings of protection, confidence and security.

These are the colors that I have found to be most directly effective. You can experiment with other colors, shades, and hues to see whether any work better for you.

Some examples of thoughtform colors in operation will help you understand the how and why of projecting them. First, I teach anyone who is going to speak or perform before an audience to energize (build up enthusiastic emotion), picture a successful outcome, and then project a pink light onto the audience. We use the pink light so often, usually in the form of a fog, that we have developed a verb, "to pinkfog." The image is that of a pink fog rolling through a room and coloring the people, furniture, walls, and everything else.

My wife, who has been an institutional consultant, used this technique quite successfully in her work. Whenever there was a problem in interdepartmental relationships, she would gather a group of aware employees and say, "Let's pinkfog the dining room (or whatever)." And she got amazing results. I used a similar technique with the color green in a business where I used to work. When I got there, the place was a rumor mill, full of back-biting, complaining, and ill feeling. After I penetrated green light through all the offices for three months, it was a pleasant place to work. The boss even came up to me one day and said, "I don't know why, but ever since you came to work here, the whole operation runs smoother than it ever has." What my wife and I and those I have taught can do, you can do, too.

Color projection has a number of other practical applications. Foremost among them is the projection of a protective influence. Many people suffer from needless anxiety about their loved ones when they are away. This is particularly the case with mothers and their children. Rather than waste all that energy worrying about the terrible things that might happen, which actually has the effect of beaming out those conditions as a suggestion, I offer a technique that will bring you more peace of mind while at the same time giving the person you care about substantial help:

Concentrate on an image of the person and mentally surround them with a cloud, fog, or light of white or gold with the quality of harmony. Instead of worrying yourself sick and doing possible harm with your imaginings, now you are able to take positive action wherever the person may be. While it sounds simple, I assure you that it is very effective. In many, many cases reported to me by my students, it has helped a person either to completely avoid unfortunate incidents or to greatly reduce the effect of unavoidable situations. And it sure helps you, the sender, to get rid of false ideas of helplessness.

Color is only one small aspect of thoughtform creation. Like miming, anything you imagine in your mind can be imagined in the outer world as well with good effect. I have used this method of thoughtform creation to make a wall to block my cat from coming into my bedroom, to make a wolf scare a mean dog away, to pet dogs at a distance to make them stop barking, to calm down an angry crowd, to reserve a parking place, to divert a stream of water, to beat my eldest son at arm wrestling, to do a whole lot of healing, and for many other practical things. However, the same rules that apply to telepathy apply to thoughtform projection. Whatever you create has to be accepted by whomever or whatever you are trying to influence, or it will have no effect.

SUMMARY

To summarize, here are the main points to remember about developing the ability to see auras and working with them:

1. Anyone can learn to see the aura with very little practice.
2. Proof of the existence of the aura lies in ancient art, modern scientific discoveries, and personal experience.
3. The basic technique for seeing the aura is
   a. find a plain or light background;
   b. hold your hand half a foot away from it;
   c. focus your gaze in the air between your fingers and around the tips of the fingers, looking for a hazy light and a dark line next to the skin.
4. The basic technique for increasing the intensity and size of the aura is to do one or all of the following:
   a. take three deep, slow breaths;

b. imagine that your aura is getting brighter and larger;

c. imagine a ball of light on top of your head filling you with energy.

5. The basic technique for projecting your aura is to imagine it surrounding something or someone with a color appropriate to your intent.

6. The basic technique for creating a thoughtform is to vividly imagine an object or scene in your external environment with as much 3-D realism as you can, and with a strong intention for it to accomplish something.

Chapter 8

The Reality of Telekinesis

O ne of people's favorite scenes in science fiction and fantasy movies is when one or more of the characters display the ability to move or lift objects with the power of thought alone. For dramatic effect, the character involved usually points a finger or faces a palm toward the object (otherwise the audience wouldn't know who was moving it). Is this just a way of pandering to popular wishful thinking, or is using thought to move things a real ability that can be developed? A hefty bit of both, I think.

The most common term for this phenomenon is *psychokinesis*, meaning "to move objects remotely by mental influence." Also referred to as PK, it was coined in 1914 by author Henry Holt and used by parapsychologist J. B. Rhine in 1934 for his famous experiments on mental influence in dice rolls. However, my own experiences have led me to prefer the older term *telekinesis* (TK), coined in 1890 by Russian researcher Alexander N. Aksakof, because it means "remote influencing" without the necessary implication that the mind alone is used. My preference notwithstanding, neither term is adequate to cover the field, which includes levitation, bending metal objects without the use of muscles or machines, and poltergeist effects, as well as remote influencing of many kinds, including healing without the intervention of a physical substance or object.

The scientific/objective worldview has a terrible time with the whole idea of TK, because it apparently flaunts the laws of physics. On the other hand, there was a time when heavier-than-air flight, running a mile in under four minutes, and traveling to the moon were also thought to flaunt the laws of physics. Actually, I hope to persuade you in this chapter that TK falls well within the laws of physics.

Although some scientists accept the phenomenon of TK as being real, many others are so rabidly against it that they insist that any examples of it must be due to fakery, mistaken perception, or some sort of hallucination or mass hypnosis (both of the latter being very unscientific explanations).

In spite of the fact that we are working with second-level assumptions now instead of first-level ones, the issue of fakery has to be acknowledged. Modern stage and street magic have become very sophisticated, and many real esper talents can be faked by professional magicians. For example, you can buy the techniques and gadgets for creating the illusion of levitation online at www.levitation.org, and the results are very convincing. However, just because you can create the illusion of a flower growing doesn't mean that flowers don't grow. You can also find a "scientifically approved" type of levitation using superconductors at www.fys.uio.no/super/levitation. However, again, just because you can create an effect by using objective-level assumptions doesn't mean you can't create a similar effect using the assumptions of other worldviews.

REVEALING THE MYSTERY
OF MIND POWER

One objection that scientists have to the possibility of producing TK effects with the power of the mind is that the brain—and many scientists believe the mind to be no more than a side effect of the brain—does not have enough energy output to be measurable more than about a meter from the body. The conclusion, therefore, is that using the mind for any TK phenomena is against the laws of physics. The problem here has nothing to do with the laws of physics or even the objective worldview. The problem is one of thinking inside the box.

In some of my workshops I demonstrate the power of mind over matter very easily. All I do is ask someone to hand me a pen and then I say, "Ta Da! With the power of my mind I have caused this pen to appear in my hand." It usually gets a laugh, but when I say this I am not joking. It all has to do with the physics of energy. To say that the mind does not have enough energy to influence an object at a distance is like saying that a match does not have enough energy to burn down a forest. Of course the match *by itself* does not have enough energy to burn down a forest, but all it has to do is to start a little fire so that the little fire can ignite something with the power to create a bigger fire, and on and on it goes. The match doesn't burn the forest down, but the forest burns down because of the match.

In my workshop example, just a few simple, mentally directed words create a very small wave in the air that has very little energy, but that wave reaches across the distance to an ear and stimulates a mental pattern of cooperation that stimulates emotional energy that stimulates the movement of muscles that results in a hand reaching out to give me a pen.

Telekinesis works in the same way. Mental energy stimulates emotional energy that influences other kinds of energy. In my experience, emotional energy is the key factor. With that out of the way, let's explore some of the phenomena associated with TK.

LEVITATION

Levitation in the second worldview generally refers to the ability of a human being to lift another person or object off the ground without direct physical contact or the use of any physical device. When one does it to oneself, it is usually called "self-levitation." I think this definition is too limited.

To me, it makes more sense to include any kind of lifting that goes beyond what can be normally expected by muscles alone.

In my considered opinion, some of the best examples of levitation in the world today can be found on professional basketball courts and among some ballet performers. If you have any doubt about this, I recommend that you compare basketball videos of the 1960s with those of today. I think the images will speak for themselves.

There are many accounts of levitation from around the world attributed to mystics, shamans, ceremonial magicians, and spiritualists, but the sources become very elusive when you try to track them down. In all my travels around the world, I have never come across a single instance of anyone just floating off the ground and hanging in mid-air for as long as they want. Just because I haven't seen it doesn't mean it doesn't happen, of course, but remarkably few people have reported witnessing such events.

That being the case, I will have to restrict my examples and techniques to what I choose to call the "levitation effect." In doing so I may draw from examples that I have reported elsewhere.

Assisted Levitation

I will list six examples of assisted levitation, three of which are easily replicable.

The Fight that Did Happen
As a sergeant in the U.S. Marine Corps, I was in charge of a work detail digging trenches. One of the men was a slacker with a smart mouth who wouldn't obey orders. After one particularly irritating comment, I suddenly gave him an uppercut to the chin. As I recall the incident, when my fist connected with his chin, it felt like a very light touch. In any case, his whole body left the ground and flew backward six or seven feet (two meters), where he landed on his back. Then he jumped up with no apparent harm and came at me with a shovel. The whole thing ended with no one getting hurt.

The Fight that Didn't Happen
After I finished military service, when I was in my second year of college, I shared an apartment with two other young men, one of whom had very irritating habits. One night when I was trying to study, he insisted on sitting next to me while he noisily snacked on potato chips. After a few attempts at politely getting him to stop, I leaped off the couch and shouted at him, burning with anger. He leaped up, too, and during the shouting match, he moved his fist toward my chest as if to punch me. As I remember it, I was highly charged with emotional energy, and before his fist touched me I flew backward across the room in a horizontal line about ten feet away from him. He suddenly became quiet, turned around, and left the room. I was experiencing an intense tingling in and around my body, and it took a very long time for that to dissipate.

The One-Inch Punch

In California when my eldest son was about twelve years old, I was studying the martial art of Bruce Lee and decided to experiment with his "One-inch Punch" technique. This consisted of being able to concentrate all of your energy into one fist and move that fist against an opponent only one inch in order to knock him backward. Using my son as a subject, I had him hold a thick telephone book against his stomach while I stood in front of him. I concentrated my energy in my right fist, moved it quickly one inch against the book, and he flew off his feet and backward about five feet (less than two meters) onto his back, but was not hurt. As I recall, it felt like I barely touched the book.

The Group Chair Lift

There are many, many variations used to produce this effect, but I will mention only one of the most simple and effective. Instead of a narrative, I will describe it as a series of steps so that you can try it, too. To do it you need five people.

1. Place a chair in an open space. Use a chair with four legs and areas under each of the four corners of the seat where someone can grasp it firmly with two hands. Use a chair that one person can lift without much trouble.

2. Pick one medium-sized person, man or woman, to sit in the chair. As a general guideline, the heavier the chair, the lighter the person should be, and vice versa.

3. Have two women grasp the front part of the chair frame under the seat and two men grasp the back part.
4. Tell the people holding the corners to lift the chair, and note how high they lift it.
5. Ask the lifters to stop, stand up, and remember some very happy moment from the past. You only need to give them ten to fifteen seconds for this. Include the person sitting in the chair if you like.
6. Suddenly tell the lifters to bend down and lift. Note how high the chair goes. Ask each person involved what they experienced.

Almost always the second lift will go significantly higher, and almost always every person involved will say that the chair felt much lighter. In some demonstrations of this type, the facilitator uses heavy breathing to increase the energy, but I find that positive emotions are better and faster.

The Single Lift
You can do this yourself or have a group of individuals do it. Use an object between five and ten pounds (two to four kilos) and lift it without any preparation. Then think of a happy moment and lift it again. The happier the feeling, the more dramatic the effect.

The Jumping Jack
Stand under something that is about a foot (thirty cm) taller than your highest standing reach. Jump up and try

to touch it. Then get as excited as you can about something good and jump again. Note the difference. It will usually be considerable, again depending on the intensity of the feeling.

BENDING METAL

I have witnessed the occurrence of bending metal many times, done it myself, and taught it to others in workshops, classes, and individual sessions. In fact, my theory of the emotional energy factor came out of my experiences with this phenomenon.

Quite a few years ago I had the opportunity to work with an emotionally troubled young man. He was what is called in parapsychology a "PK (or TK) agent," that is, someone around whom poltergeist-type phenomena occur. His father taught spoon bending, which is a possible reason why this young man's talent took on the characteristics it did.

When I visited the young man's home, I was shown two examples of "poltergeist" activity. In one case, during the young man's fit of anger, the thick bars of a cast-iron fire grate and the cast-iron tools that went with it flopped over as if they were made of licorice. The second case happened when he was on the phone with his girlfriend and she cancelled a date. As he slammed down the phone, there was a big crashing sound in the kitchen. At first nothing unusual could be found, but when three drawers of kitchen utensils were opened it could be seen that every item in them was bent. However, they were not bent equally: the items in the drawer nearest the phone were only bent a little bit, in the next drawer they were bent a great deal, and in the third drawer they were only bent a little bit. With all three drawers open, the effect looked exactly like a wave. That's when I began theorizing that emotional energy was involved in such phenomena and that it moved outward from the individual in waves, with more intense emotions creating waves of higher amplitude.

One time when I was helping the young man to redirect his emotions, he called me to his bedroom to show me something. There he was, sitting on the floor, holding the end of a thick bar of hardened copper about a foot (thirty cm) long. As I watched, he stared at the rod and it slowly began to droop as if it had turned soft. If I hadn't known about his intense emotional energy, it would have seemed like he was merely using his mind. He eventually became a healer, and later, as his emotional problems were resolved, his talent faded away, he got married, and led a normal life.

In my personal experience, I was never able to bend metal with pure emotion. Like most "spoon-benders," I added a little bit of physical pressure. It was a strange experience. Although I had been told to stroke the metal and will it or ask it to bend, I found that wasn't necessary. What was necessary was that I increase my level of emotional intensity. As I held the spoon, fork, or knife and concentrated my attention and energy on it, it would suddenly, in spurts, soften enough that only a slight pressure from my fingers would cause it to bend. Then it would suddenly harden and I would have to build up my emotional intensity again until it would suddenly soften for a bit and I could bend it more.

As a result of many experiments, I determined that silver was the easiest to bend, then copper, and then steel. Interestingly, this is also the descending order of electrical conductivity. When I could not find enough real silverware for a workshop I was doing, I used hardened copper hangers employed by carpenters to hold joists, and they worked very well. I remember the shock on one man's face when he picked up his sweet and gentle wife after the workshop and she showed him her intricately twisted piece of hardened copper that he couldn't bend with all his strength.

MOVING OBJECTS

The ability to move objects without touching them is rarely encountered, if we don't count the ability to ask or order someone else to do it for us. Most of the time it occurs as an unintentional, spontaneous event.

The most well-known cases of spontaneous TK with objects involve so-called "poltergeist" activity. The name, from Germany, means "noisy ghost," which reflects the idea that spirits or ghosts of some kind are responsible.

Many parapsychological researchers, including myself, are now convinced that the sudden and often violent movement of objects is due to a PK/TK agent, a particular person who is always around when the phenomenon occurs. Usually this is a boy or girl around the age of puberty, but cases have been reported that involve much younger or much older people, as well. While the aforesaid researchers have a tendency to say that the event has occurred by "means unknown," I am convinced that a sudden, unconscious release of emotional energy is what does it.

Typical effects are that objects around the person will rattle, tumble off surfaces, or even fly off rapidly in all directions. I know of one case, though, when instead of objects flying away from the agent, rocks from outdoors bombarded the house he was in from all sides.

Unfortunately, I know of only one person who made the transition from PK/TK agent to consciously controlling the process, and that was the Russian woman, Nina Kulagina, who lived from 1926 to 1990. She noticed that objects near her would rattle and fall when she was in an angry mood, and she decided that the effect was coming from her and not from anyone or anything else. At that point she began to consciously develop TK as a skill. She gave many demonstrations of her ability to consciously move objects without touching them. Some of these were strictly controlled to avoid fakery, and some were filmed. Naturally, objective worldview scientists insisted and continue to insist that the events had to be faked, and TK researchers keep saying it was done "only with her mind." If you read careful descriptions of what she actually did, however, you get the indication that something else was involved.

Descriptions by witnesses say that she needed hours of preparation to clear her mind and concentrate; she would know she was ready when she got a sharp pain in her spine and her eyes blurred. Nevertheless, all she was ever able to do in her known demonstrations was to move small objects a short distance across a surface. Her conscious skill, while remarkable in its own way, never reached the level of her unconscious effects.

Personal Experiences

My experiences moving objects nonphysically have been somewhat limited but definite. Among my family members, only my younger brother ever reported anything like this. Once, he told me, he was at a meeting and strongly wanted a particular letter on the conference table that was out of his reach. Instantly, the paper flew into his hand. No one else at the table appeared to notice.

I cannot remember any truly spontaneous experiences of my own—except one with a Crookes radiometer that I obtained for the purpose of doing TK experiments. A Crookes radiometer is a hermetically sealed glass globe with most of the air removed from the interior. Inside the globe is a low-friction spindle on which are mounted four thin metal vanes painted black on one side and white on the other. As sunlight, flashlight beams, or infrared or heat radiation strike the vanes, differences in temperature between the white and black sides cause the vanes to rotate. Warm hands placed on the globe can also have this effect, but hands just a few inches or centimeters from the globe do not. I had been trying for some time to cause the vanes to move without touching the globe but had had no success. Then one day I happened to be standing about a foot away from the radiometer when I received some tremendously exciting news. Feeling as if I was bursting with emotion, I suddenly turned and stared at the radiometer, and the vanes began spinning. The effect lasted less than a minute, but it was dramatic.

I had an intentional experience with another object. In a closed room about fifteen feet (less than five meters) square, with no draft, I suspended a lightweight statuette of a pelican by a nylon thread from an overhead rafter. The wingspan of the bird was just short of one foot (thirty cm). Seated in a chair or on the floor some six or seven feet away (two meters), I was able, after some practice, to cause the bird to spin slowly in one direction and then reverse the direction before the thread had wound to its limit. My technique, if you can call it that, was to get very relaxed, very concentrated, and then will the bird to move, being careful not to allow any muscles to tense up.

My best experiences came as a result of reading a book by Claude M. Bristol entitled *The Magic of Believing*

(Pocket Books, 1948; Touchstone, 1991). In chapter 2, "Mind-Stuff Experiments," he describes an extremely simple device for demonstrating TK that stunned me by its effectiveness. I modified his design a little to make it more portable and gave demonstrations in schools and on television. Years later, I came upon a manufactured version of the device that worked equally well, but I don't know if it is still available. At any rate, my simple version can still be used by anyone. First, the instructions on how to make it:

1. Obtain a paper cup, the kind with a flat bottom. If it has a little ridge around the rim, that's okay.
2. Place the cup upside down on a flat surface.
3. Cut a square of paper about three inches (eight cm) on a side. Twenty-pound paper or the kind used for ink-jet printers works fine.
4. Fold the paper twice, corner to corner, so you end up with something that resembles the top of a square tent.
5. Obtain a Gem plastic push pin and set it upside down on the base of the cup. Place the paper tent on top of the pin, balanced so that it hangs evenly. Now you are ready.

Make sure the device is placed at a comfortable height on a table or desk in front of you. Place your hands, palms inward, about four inches (ten cm) away from the paper on either side. Keep your mouth closed and breathe very gently, so that your breath doesn't stir the paper accidentally. Actually, when the paper starts to move you will be able to tell the difference between breath movement and energy movement very easily.

For some people, the paper will begin to spin immediately, sometimes with a little wobble. For others, it won't move no matter what they do. For still others, it will spin a little and stop; and for others, it will spin a little one way, then reverse itself.

Muscle relaxation is vital, except that sometimes you can quickly squeeze your muscles hard and get a short burst of movement. I have found that taking a break to walk around, breathe deeply, and get excited about something before trying again can be very helpful. With practice you can get better and better at making the paper spin in either direction. The three most important factors, in my opinion, are muscle relaxation, emotional excitement, and the ability to concentrate your will without tensing up.

So now you can make a piece of paper spin. So what?

Assisted Movement of Objects

There is not a great deal of value in bending spoons or making a paper tent spin around, but there is a great value in applying the abilities involved to other things.

Rather than wasting your time just trying to move things with only your mind (which doesn't work) or with only your emotional energy (which works in a limited way unless you can conjure up an extremely strong emotional state, which then becomes hard to control), all you have to do is add the magic of physical energy.

This is what most people do with spoon bending. Effectively done, the emotional energy softens the metal enough that a little physical pressure can make the metal bend. The same thing happened with the chair lift, the object lift, and the enhanced jumping. What I'm proposing now is that you learn to add mentally directed emotional energy to any physical thing that you do. Here's a short list of uses to which I've put this idea:

- With a group of people, I pushed a car up a steep hill with the help of emotional energy; we could not budge it with just physical force.
- While clearing land, I pulled saplings out of the ground and tossed heavy roots onto a far pile for hours without strain.
- I opened hard-to-open packages and jars with ease.
- I repaired a car radio by charging the condenser with emotional energy.
- I applied emotional energy to thousands of healings.
- I won an arm-wrestling contest by creating a thought-form of an atomic engine with a titanium steel rod attached to my wrist that pulled my arm over easily.
- I won a canoe race by focusing emotional energy into a pair of thoughtform dolphins that pushed us ahead to victory.

- I almost won a game of horseshoes. This is a game where players compete by tossing real horseshoes toward a distant pin. The horseshoes that land closest to the pin earn points, and, if one is a "ringer"—meaning that it ends up encircling the pin—it earns extras points.

The last item presents us with an ethical conundrum. In a sporting event, is it ethical to try to make another player make a mistake by using knowledge that he or she may not have? This occurs in a lot of sports by withholding knowledge that might benefit the other player, but what about using knowledge that would decrease the other player's chance of winning? I know that is done all the time without question in contact sports like martial arts and boxing, but what about non-contact sports?

Let me use the horseshoe game as an illustration of what I mean. I was playing with a group of strangers, plus a few people I did know but not well, and I hadn't played horseshoes for at least twenty years. So I decided to add some TK to the event, without advertising what I was doing.

Each time another player got ready to toss a horseshoe I would concentrate my attention and my energy on the person's throwing hand just at the moment before the toss, and then I would give it a sort of mental twist. I didn't do this all the time, but, every time I did, the horseshoe would be tossed significantly off course. The critical factor in this experiment was the other person's degree of concentration. Most people who aren't experts at something do not concentrate very well no matter what they are doing. However, my "talent" would work only if I exerted my twist at the last moment before the other players let go, when their physical force was greatest and their concentration was the lowest. It was then that they were most likely to react with a slight twitch of the wrist, which would send the horseshoe flying farther away from the target.

We played off in pairs and I was doing very well. Not only was I "helping" my competitors to miss the target, but I was also focusing a beam of energy for my horseshoe to follow, and I was making more ringers than I ever had before in my life.

However, the final match was between me and a horseshoe champion. Nothing I did could divert his concentration, and in the end he won the game by one point because he was simply a better player.

So, I've decided to resolve my ethical dilemma by revealing the secret of how to counteract the TK supplement if it is ever used against you. Keep your confidence, your presence, and your concentration, and it won't have any effect on you. If you ever play a game with me, we'll see how well you've practiced.

Part 4

Changing Reality in
the Symbolic World

Lives

I have trod the tiled walkways
Of a temple in Tibet,
Raised a sacrifice to Isis on the Nile;

As a priest in Mayan feathers
I have praised the Sun and Moon,
Macchu Picchu was my homeland for awhile.

Midst the gods of old Hawaii
I commanded fire and rain,
In Atlantis I moved ships across the sea.

As an Austrian alchemist
I turned base lead into gold,
And in China followed Tao and studied chi.

All the lives that I have lived and
All the mem'ries I have stored
Rest within me as they wait to be set free;

And maybe that will happen
And maybe not at all,
'Cause maybe I'll just dream another me.

—Serge Kahili King, 1974

Chapter 9

Tripping through the Land of Dreams

D reams are no more than brain static, undigested remnants of yesterday's real events, or dramatized fears and wishes; and for the most part it is a waste of time to pay attention to them, according to objective reality. Dreams are memories of the past, divinations of the future, doorways for mind control, or messages from spirit guides, according to subjective reality.

Following the assumptions of symbolic reality, though, dreams are obviously symbols. Symbols of what? Of reality, of course. And since the basic assumption of this worldview is that everything is a symbol, then reality is a symbol and symbols are reality. Therefore, all our daily world is symbolic and dreams are real.

HOW REAL IS REAL?

One of the little mind-expanding things I like to do in some of my workshops is to have everyone in the audience remember a dream. Then I have everyone remember a vacation. Then I challenge anyone to tell me the difference between the two events as *memories*, disregarding content and emotions. Invariably, when treated as memories, no one can. Which forces the question, how do you tell what is real and what's not?

The answer certainly does not depend upon sensory intensity. Another mind-expander I do sometimes is have the audience remember a dream and then remember lunch two weeks ago Tuesday. Unless it was a very dramatic lunch or unless someone takes a long time to create a sequence of associated memories, the lunch memory is so dim it might as well never have happened, and the dream recalled seems much more real by comparison.

Some people insist that the nature of the content of the experience, if not the content itself, is the deciding factor for what is real. After all, dreams are weird. Things happen in dreams that can't happen in "real life." This is a poor argument, because a lot of weird things happen in "real life" and a lot of "realistic" things happen in dreams. We'll explore some of those weird things that occur in "real life" in a later chapter.

In spite of the fact that we cannot distinguish between the memories of dream events and "real" events qualitatively, we certainly do so quantitatively. That which we are used to calling "real" is distinguished primarily by the greater number of fairly consistent memories we have of it. On the other hand, because both kinds of events are indistinguishable in terms of quality, and because dreams seem as real as ordinary reality does when you are experiencing them, ordinary reality—or outer experience, as some call it—is considered by the symbolic worldview to be another dream. This does not mean that life as we know it is an illusion, for in the symbolic worldview, all dreams are real experiences.

WHY DOES IT MATTER?

The relation between dreams and outer reality wouldn't matter except for one very important fact ("fact" being something that can be experienced by all human beings). In addition to being symbolic and real at the same time, all dreams are connected by their related symbols. A resulting practical consequence is that if you change one dream, all related dreams change.

We all know that when we make changes in our outer life, our dream life changes. What shamans know, and what I'm going to teach you about, is that the converse is also true: when we make changes in our dream life, our *outer* life changes. And that has profound implications for the purpose of this book, since changing dreams is far more useful than interpreting them.

THE INTERPRETATION COMPULSION

The first thing many people want to know when they remember a dream is, "What does it mean?" As a result, an impressive number of books on dream interpretation have been published, and some kinds of psychotherapists have built their entire careers around it.

Well, I'm not saying that dream interpretation can't be useful. It's just not as useful as other ways of working with dreams. If you'd like some ideas on dream interpretation that are not bound by the dogma of one particular system, I suggest that you read the chapter on "Dream Talk" in my book *Mastering Your Hidden Self* and the chapter on "Changing the World with Shaman Dreaming" in *Urban Shaman*. Meanwhile, here are a few ideas on dream interpretation that did not make it into those books.

1. Regardless of anything else it might represent, the dream you dream is always about you. It *might* be about someone or something else, but it is *always* about you.
2. The best source for dream interpretation is the dream itself. I mention this briefly in *Urban Shaman*, but here is the information again in steps:
   a. Recall the dream, or any part of the dream.
   b. Assume that everything in the dream is alive, aware, and responsive.

    c. Ask each object in the dream what it represents and why it is there.

    d. Accept whatever you see, hear, or feel as the object's *opinion* of why it is there and what it represents. Reserve your own right to believe it or not.

    e. If you don't get any response, assume that the object doesn't know and that therefore it isn't important for you to know.

In spite of the potential usefulness of interpreting dreams, it is an extremely restrictive way of working with them, and the reason is that verbal language by itself is so restrictive. Still another mind expander that I use is to ask an audience if anyone is familiar with classical music and with Beethoven's Fifth Symphony in particular. There are usually a small number who are. I then ask one of them to describe the symphony to the rest of the audience using words. The typical response is a blank stare, a rueful smile, and a helpless shrug of the shoulders.

The fact is that music is a language that doesn't translate well into words. Art is also a language that defies accurate verbal translation (some of the attempts are hilariously absurd, even to the artists). The same problem exists with taste and smell and dance. Words can be translated rather well into other forms of communication, but not the other way around. For that matter, translating one verbal language into another can present insurmountable challenges. Idioms are almost impossible to translate accurately, and some concepts aren't translatable, even between related languages. When I teach in Germany, I always use a translator, and over the years I've picked up enough German to sometimes know what the translator is saying. On one occasion, I was speaking about physical aches and pains and I heard the translator say, in German, "pains and pains." Afterward I learned that *ache*, which in English means a specific type of pain, has no real counterpart in German and has to be translated as *pain*. I do my best now to avoid that phrase whenever I'm speaking in Germany, Switzerland, or Austria.

All of this brings us to the point of recognizing that symbols are a language unto themselves and, like music, cannot be rendered accurately or well into verbal language. The compulsion to do so is an effect of our obsession with words as the most important form of communication we have in the modern world. The way symbols are usually interpreted is something like interpreting a musical composition as "stirring," "sweet," or "airy." It leaves out most of the experience.

The elements of a dream are representations of highly intricate patterns of ideas, beliefs, and expectations. When these are representations of fear, anger, or disharmony, we have the possibility of using the symbolic language to resolve the symbolic problem and thereby heal the underlying complex patterns. If I may use a verbal analogy: when you write a letter and the words you choose result in your message being misunderstood, the problem can usually be resolved by changing the words.

CHANGE THE SYMBOLS AND
CHANGE YOUR LIFE

The basic process for using symbols to change reality is to create a symbol of a condition or situation that needs changing and then change the symbol. If that sounds too simple, it is.

Let me explain the process more thoroughly. First, you create a symbol with your focus mind. Usually the symbol comes into being by willing, wanting, wishing, or asking for it. The source of the symbol is your body mind, which draws upon memories, patterns of personal beliefs and expectations, current sensory awareness, and connections through your energy field with any other related source of information.

Next, you change the symbol in some way. By this I do NOT mean that you replace it. The symbol is an expression of the whole complex issue, or at least whatever part of it you are able to access right now, so simply replacing it with another symbol doesn't accomplish anything. The key to effectiveness in symbol changing is to work with the presenting symbol and change its appearance, structure, content, or position. Since it is a product of your body mind, you have to change it in a way that influences your body mind. That means you use your complete sensory imagination to redo the symbol so that your body mind makes equivalent changes throughout the entire network it drew from to create the symbol in the first place.

179

There is no way for your focus mind to understand the process, any more than you can understand how the words come to you when you speak or sing. You can, however, know when your symbol changing has an effect, because your body mind will react with some kind of tension release (relaxing, sighing, etc.) or change of energy state (tingling, current, expansion, pleasure, etc.). By the same token, some kinds of changes that you try may result in increased tension or unpleasant feelings, and those signals are indications for you to do something different. All in all, your body provides the feedback.

If you are using symbol change for personal healing, you may experience immediate feedback in the form of some degree of change in the physical condition. For other kinds of conditions or situations, the feedback may take longer to be apparent. In general, the more people involved, the longer it may take and the smaller the effect may be. Sometimes it seems as if the initial symbol change affects only one layer or piece of the complex, so further symbol work may be necessary for better results.

Now let us start working with techniques.

Exterior Symbols

To begin, I want to make clear that I am not talking about gazing at printed or drawn symbols in order to go into an altered state of consciousness. That may have its benefits, but it is not the topic of this discussion. Here we are concerned only with ways of working with symbols that will help change our inner *and* outer reality. There are two kinds of exterior symbols that will be discussed in this section: symbols made from physical objects and symbols created as thoughtforms.

Physical Symbols

Any group of seven or more objects will do. There is nothing special about the number seven in this context except that it seems to be the minimum number for producing some kind of reasonably complex pattern. Sticks, stones, crystals, or any objects approximately one-half inch to one inch (1.25 cm to 2.5 cm) in length or diameter will be fine. My favorite set consists of fifty fairly small cowrie shells that I keep in a pouch. When I want to use them, I just pour a handful into my palm without bothering to count them.

Whatever you use, hold the items in your hand and think about the condition or situation you want to change. Give yourself about a minute to keep it in your awareness as neutrally as possible, accepting that whatever it is, it is true only for the moment. When you are ready, guided by your intuition, toss the objects out in front of you and look at the pattern they form. Remember that you are not trying to interpret the pattern, so it doesn't matter if it looks like anything you recognize or not. Instead of interpreting, then, you want to try to "feel" the pattern with your aura. If that sounds too abstract, just gaze at the pattern and be aware of any physical or emotional sensations that occur. When you are ready, start modifying the pattern until it looks or feels better. The results are more profound if you do your best to move the individual pieces as little as you can in order to gain the effect you want. Keep this up until you have a pattern that both looks and feels good to you. Sometimes your body will even produce a spontaneous sigh, positive emotion, or energy sensation at this point. That's the signal that you've done all you can do for this session. The results may or may not be immediately apparent, but something in the condition or situation will change. There is no rule about how many times you can cast and change a symbol.

Just now I tossed my cowrie shells on a nearby glass table while focusing on a situation to change. I haven't received a telephone call from any family member for three days. My wife is helping a colleague with a workshop and doesn't call me during the day. Although I like the quiet, I decided to change the situation. I held the shells, thinking about the fact that no one had called, accepting it as a temporary experience, and then I cast the shells. The first thing I do with cowrie shells is make sure all of them are turned with the hump up. The pattern was confusing, but I could see some potential, so I moved different pieces bit by bit until there was a sort of circle with a small spiral inside that felt very good. Then I put them away and went back to typing. A half-hour later, my wife called about something with which she normally would not have bothered, especially during a training.

Thoughtform Symbols

Do you recall the work we did with second worldview thoughtforms? Then we were creating energetic simulations of real objects to produce realistic effects. Now we are doing something different. This time you are asking your body mind to create a symbol of an existing condition or situation in the outer world so that it can be perceived by your focus mind's eye. For instance, at the time of writing this book, I was trying to sell a house. When I asked my body mind to project a symbol onto the floor of the office where I'm typing this, I "saw" a house about two feet (sixty cm) high covered in heavy chains. I could have guessed what that meant, but I didn't need to know. What I did was to imagine a cutting torch with a green flame (green is a symbol of love for me) and I cut the chains away. As they fell to the ground they turned into fertilizer for the landscaping, and the house began to glow with happiness. Finally, a little bar of floating text appeared above the house that read "New Owner." While that felt good, it didn't seem like enough. Shortly afterward, my wife and I did an additional symbol ritual at the house. That ritual consisted of symbolizing each room of the house as a person, sharing good memories of things that happened in the room, and saying good-bye. The house sold a week later for cash.

If you find it too difficult simply to have an image appear in front of you, try this: Make or draw a black circle on white paper like I described in the chapter on telepathic receiving. Gaze at it until you get some kind of energetic response (visual or kinesthetic), and then ask for a symbol of a condition or situation to appear within the circle. After you get one, even if it appears in your mind instead of in the circle, use your conscious imagination to change it until it pleases you.

Exterior thoughtform symbols can appear anywhere in your environment, even over the heads of people or inside things. Also, they do not have to be single images. They may also appear as scenes or "dreamlets," as I described in the chapter on dreams in *Urban Shaman*.

Unstructured Interior Symbols

The simplest form of working with unstructured interior symbols is to think of a condition or situation, ask for a symbol, let it appear in your mind, and change it as described above.

Tune in to a Dream

A much more interesting form is to assume, in a third worldview context, that everything dreams, and then you just tune in to the dream. I also brought up this idea in *Urban Shaman*, but I'll cover it in more detail here as a series of steps in a practice exercise:

1. Relax in a comfortable place and close your eyes. I recommend doing this exercise in a chair or in a

seated posture, because it is much harder to hold your focus while lying down. Two or three deep breaths will help.

2. Think of your brain and ask to know what it is dreaming. Trust that whatever you get *is* the dream of your brain at the present moment, whether it is a moving or static scene, a single image, a memory, something abstract, a color, or nothing. Just be aware of it for about thirty seconds.

3. Shift your attention to your heart and ask to be aware of its dream.

4. Shift your attention to your liver and ask to be aware of its dream.

5. Go back to each organ, starting with the brain. Whether the dream is the same or not, good or not, use your conscious imagination to make it better than it is, using the elements of the dreams as a starting point. Stay with the dream of each organ until you get a good feeling from the changes you've made.

6. Come back to self-awareness, wiggle your fingers and toes, take a deep breath, and open your eyes.

Night Dreams

I won't go into night dreams very deeply because I think I covered the subject well in *Urban Shaman*. The basic premise is that you change dreams of anger, fear, or disharmony as described above. What I will do here is just reiterate a few important points.

1. The easiest way to work with night dreams is after the fact, with the memory of the dream. The sooner you work with the memory of the dream, the sooner you get the benefits of any changes you make. Nevertheless, you can work productively with childhood dreams when you are an adult because the memories still exist now and the patterns they represent are still active, unless you've already changed them.

2. There are three primary ways to work effectively with dream symbols:

   a. Pick any point in the dream and change your reaction to what's happening.

   b. Pick any point in the dream and change the story so it turns out good.

   c. Allow the dream to continue past the worst part (usually the part that woke you up) until it resolves itself. Even as a memory, the story will change on its own; and even if it gets worse for a while, it will eventually and inevitably resolve itself into a good ending. However, you may or may not want to wait that long.

3. Remember to introduce helping agents of your own choosing into your dream, changing when you feel stuck. These can be fairies, elves, angels, heroes, friends, animals, or whatever.

4. The sooner you can teach this practice to children, the sooner you can help them deal with the issues behind nightmares in a healthy, enjoyable way that increases their self-esteem and self-confidence.

Dream Structures

Now we enter the area of shamanic dreaming, an area of vast differences in cultural practices and in theoretical explanations. We'll begin by noting similarities shared by shamans of all times and places.

1. All shamans use a more or less formalized structure in which to do their dream work, a particular dream environment in which the change work takes place.
2. All of them move through that environment on what has come to be called a "shamanic journey" of short or long duration.
3. All of them do this dream work for the purpose of learning, healing, or empowering themselves or others.
4. All of them encounter and interact with other beings of various types.
5. All of them accept without a doubt that these experiences are as real, and sometimes more real, than experiences in the "outer" world.
6. All of them are so focused on the "journey" experience that they appear to others to be in a light to deep trance, whether they are sitting, standing, or moving.

And that's about it.

Apart from culture, which may be expressed in costume, language, ritual, and descriptions of the inner world, one of the greatest differences in shamanic dreaming is in how shamans get there. In some cultures, shamans use drums of various sorts; some use whistles, some use drugs, some use dance, some use rattles, some use combinations of those, and some just do it. By that I mean they enter the shamanic environment simply by shifting their attention there. Examples of the latter type are the shamans of Hawaii, Korea, and Mongolia (Mongolian shamans use drums, not to go into the inner world, but to energize the journey).

The important thing to know is that the only reason shamans can do this kind of dreaming is because it is a human thing to do. They may be the experts by training and/or practice, but they are only doing what all humans are capable of doing.

What I teach is the Hawaiian version as I learned it from my uncle, Wana Kahili, and it has enabled thousands of non-shamans to go on inner journeys of wonder and joy and healing.

In *Mastering Your Hidden Self*, I introduced the "Garden" structure. In *Urban Shaman*, I expanded on that and introduced the gathering place I named "Bali Hai," "Lanikeha," the place of archetypes, and also "Milu," the place of challenges. I did such a good job, I think, that I won't have to repeat that information here.

What I will do instead in the following sections is to expand the Garden work further and introduce you to Hawaiian-style Soul Retrieval.

TRIPPING THROUGH THE LAND OF DREAMS

BEYOND THE GARDEN

First, I'll present a brief review of how to enter your own personal inner space that we call "The Garden."

1. Get into a comfortable position, take a deep breath, and close your eyes.
2. Imagine a garden, any kind of garden. It could be one you remember being in, one you've seen in a picture, one you make up right now, or one that just appears.
3. See one thing in your garden as clearly as you can. This might be a tree, a flower, a rock, or anything else.
4. Hear one thing as clearly as you can, such as wind in the trees, a bee buzzing around a flower, water flowing over a rock, or anything else.
5. Touch one thing as clearly as you can, like the trunk of a tree, the petals of a flower, water flowing, or anything else.
6. Expand your awareness of your garden. What is the ground like? What kinds of plants are there? What else is around?

At this point you would normally do the things I've suggested elsewhere. For instance, you might call up a symbol to work with, invite the spirit of someone or something into your Garden to communicate with, go to Bali Hai or enter Lanikeha or Milu, or simply play and relax.

This time, however, I'm going to suggest that you go and visit someone else's Garden. Why would you want to do this?

1. To just explore and find out what another person's Garden is like.
2. To ask for a symbol of that person's problem and work on it in their own Garden.
3. To go the garden of a group, an organization, or a location and do symbol healing or empowerment.

The last suggestion might be a new idea for you, but if everything dreams, then everything also has its own Garden. In the healing circles that I lead, we often go to the Garden of Aloha International and empower it with gifts and creative symbols to help its projects be more effective. Sometimes we will also work with helping the rainforest, certain animal species like dolphins or tigers, and even cities or countries. Before we get into the process, though, we need to cover some important considerations:

1. Remember what I said about dreams? They *might* be about someone or something else, but they are *always* about you. This is true about all the dreams that come into your awareness. So you are never actually going into the dream of someone or something else, and you are never actually going into the Garden of someone or something else. It is always *your version* of their

dream or Garden. This is very important. If you ever think you need permission to go into someone else's Garden, you have fallen out of the symbolic worldview and into the subjective worldview, which will make your Garden work less effective (in the objective worldview you wouldn't even dream of having an inner Garden).

2. To remain effective in this work, you must always remember that the most you can do is to help, and your help may or may not be accepted. Whether or not your help is accepted depends on whether your brand of help matches the motivations of the person or thing you want to help. Everyone and everything has free will on some level, according to the fifth principle of Huna.

Now for the process, which is simplicity itself, once you know how to get into your own Garden.

1. After you are in your Garden, look for an exit and find a path that leads to the Garden of the person or thing you want to help. Some people prefer to ask a power animal or a spirit guide to assist them. That's up to you.

2. Once you are in the other's Garden, call up a symbol and go to work. When you are finished, give a blessing or thanks, go back to your own Garden, and then back to your ordinary reality. It isn't critical that you

end the session this way, but when you are using an inner structure it is a good idea to follow the assumptions of that structure. This helps to build a habit in your body mind that makes the process easier each time you do it.

SOUL RETRIEVAL

The way of changing reality having to do with soul retrieval is based on some shamanic assumptions that may sound strange if you've never heard them before. I'll try to put the concept into plain modern language.

When a person has experienced a traumatic event in life and seems to lose some positive quality, characteristic, talent, skill, or interest that they had before, some shamanic cultures assume that the portion of the person's consciousness containing that positive aspect has left the person by some means and has to be brought back so that the person can be restored to full consciousness. Unfortunately, modern Western translations of this concept have named the problem "soul loss" and the solution "soul retrieval." This leads to a lot of confusion because the word *soul* has many meanings. Even more unfortunately, we don't have a good single word to replace it, so I will use it in quotes only because I have to.

Naturally, different cultures that use this concept approach the problem in different ways. In cultures with a warrior type of shamanic tradition, it is generally assumed that an evil spirit of some kind has stolen the person's "soul" and, sometimes, hidden it in an object somewhere in the inner world. The shaman's role is to find the object, retrieve the "soul," bring it back to the outer world, and insert it back into the person to make them whole again. In some cultures the shaman has to do battle with the evil spirit in order to retrieve the "soul."

I was taught how to do this process from a Hawaiian perspective, which means we assume that the "soul part" left on its own because of the trauma in order to find a safer and more pleasant place to live, and it is the shaman's role to persuade it to come back.

In the objective worldview, this sounds absurd, although an objective psychologist might make a case for it as a metaphorically symbolic process. The second worldview might accept it as an event taking place in a nonmaterial world involving spirits, with the reinsertion of the soul being just a ritual. In the shamanic, or symbolic, worldview, though, it is a real event in a real world closely related to this one.

Contrary to some current teachings, however, this is not something that all shamans do every time they do a healing. It is only undertaken in special circumstances that seem to require it. Typically, shamans will use a number of other techniques to solve the problem before resorting to a "soul retrieval."

The Soul Retrieval Process

In situations where your client's problem at hand raises the possibility that "soul retrieval" might be called for, here are a series of steps for proceeding:

1. Determine that a "soul retrieval" is either the most useful way to help the client or a very useful addition to other methods.

2. Obtain a symbolic "soul sucker" and a symbolic "soul carrier." The "soul sucker" is a tubular object used to suck up the "soul" when it is found and then blow it into the client's navel in order to return it. The "soul carrier" is a symbolic object used to contain the "soul" and bring it back from the inner world to the outer world. In practice, the shaman holds physical objects during the retrieval process and uses their nonphysical counterparts during the inner journey. When he or she finds the lost "soul part," it is sucked up into the nonphysical sucker and inserted into the nonphysical carrier. On the shaman's return to the outer world, it is assumed that the "soul part" is inside the physical carrier. Then the physical sucker is used to suck it out of the carrier and blow it into the client's navel. For a "sucker" I prefer a tubular stone about three inches long that was given to me by my African shaman mentor, and for a "carrier" I use one of several globular stones from my personal collection. When

teaching others to do this during a workshop, I provide coffee stirrers and marbles, which work just as well.

3. When the client is present, narrate your journey out loud. When the client is not present, simply do the whole process in your own mind.

4. For the journey, go to your inner Garden (see above), call on a power animal or helper spirit to act as a guide, ask it to lead you to the missing "soul part," and, when you find it, however it appears, persuade it to come back by describing the benefits of a fuller life as a whole being. When it has agreed and is in the "carrier," make your way back to your Garden, thank your guide, bless your Garden, and come back to "outer world" consciousness.

5. With the client present, assume that the "soul part" is in the carrier. Suck it out, point your sucker at the client's navel, and blow it in. If appropriate, rub the client's navel area gently in a circular motion to "seal" the "soul part" in (over clothing, of course). Or, if not appropriate, make a circular gesture near the navel. Then look into the client's eyes for some kind of change, and ask the client for his or her reactions.

Since a description of the step-by-step process does not give a sense of the actual experience, I will describe several different soul retrievals: first, two examples of soul retrievals done without the client present; then a description of a personal session; and, finally, a fictional narrative from my novel *Dangerous Journeys* that was based on a real session.

The Inner Child

In this case, a baby was born with serious physical complications leading to a medical prognosis of a very short life span, even with surgery. I did a journey for the baby, assuming that a "soul part" was not willing or not interested in living a full life. With the help of a leopard power animal, I found the "soul part" in the form of a young boy living a simple but happy life in a rural village. At this time in my life, I was heavily into role-playing computer games, so I used the fun and adventure of that as an inducement for the boy to return to the body of the baby. When the "soul part" agreed, I completed the process in my own mind. (Note: shamanically, I completed the process in the inner world.) The result was that the baby survived the surgery and grew up with a passion for computer games. He is now twenty years old and a sixty-plus level player in the massive multiplayer role-playing game called *World of Warcraft*.

New Growth

"Karen" was a seven-year-old who looked and acted as if she was no older than eighteen months. At her parents' request, I did a soul retrieval to see if I could find a missing part and, if I did, persuade it to reintegrate with the physical body. I saw the girl once but did the process from a distance. This time I used an owl power animal for my guide, and, after a long search, I found the missing part in the form of an adult woman artist working in a loft in a city that resembled New York. At first she was not interested in the whole process of growing up before doing what she wanted to do, but I was able to persuade her that the process of growing up could be used as creative material for her art, and she finally agreed to return. Over the next two years, Karen showed more and more interest in her surroundings, and her body made good progress in physical growth after years of no change. I lost touch with the family after that.

A Client Describes a Personal Session

The following was told to me by a client, and I am reporting it as a first-person account.

> After reading Sandra Ingerman's book *Welcome Home*, I considered some of her thoughts about soul retrieval. I began thinking about an unusual feeling I had had for a couple of months, since before I left San Diego and my significant other (S.O.) in mid-December, and particularly since I had arrived on Kauai. In shamanic traditions all over the world, it has been held that when a person goes through a particularly traumatic event—an accident, a serious illness, the death of someone close, the loss of an important relationship, witnessing or being involved in an act of violence—the person can lose a part of his or her soul, and Ingerman discussed this in her book.

For some time I had had a sense of being in an extremely altered state. I had heard myself mention it several times to people. After coming to Kauai, some part of the feeling became even more acute. I felt lost, at times seriously so. I sensed that a large chunk of some aspect of myself was unavailable to me, and I did not have one clue about how to get it back or find it. I could not feel or sense what I was supposed to be doing—at that moment or on into the future. Phrases came to mind like, "I can't get a grip on things," or "I can't get a handle on things." I felt as though I could not find my way, and it was very frustrating and at times frightening. I remember telling my S.O. on a few occasions before I left that I really wasn't sure I could see any point or purpose in my finishing or living out the remainder of this particular life.

Four years previously I'd begun studying and training in a form of Hawaiian shamanism that includes a soul-retrieval ritual, and I began to sense that this ritual might be of great help. I decided to ask people I knew if they would be interested in assisting me. Generally speaking, the person helping goes on a shamanic journey and retrieves the missing piece or pieces of the soul and then restores it in the person needing the help. Most of the people I talked to were busy, but someone suggested that I talk to Serge Kahili King, the shaman who has taught most of the classes I've taken. Feeling a certain sense of urgency, as though my situation might be approaching a critical point, I called him, and, after discussing details of my symptomatic experience, he said that we would get together three days later and conduct the ritual with/ for me. Arranging for help allowed me to relax just slightly, which was a great relief. It was frustrating for me to be on Kauai, knowing what I know about the healing properties of this island, and to feel so separate and isolated—from the island, from myself, from everything in some strange way.

I asked for dreams that would help me with the soul retrieval, and, two nights before my appointment, I believe I had one. It included one aspect of me as a new infant and another as a tiny, perfectly formed, proud and well-dressed young man. One woman friend whom I had asked about doing the soul retrieval with me seemed to indicate that she would help me if I needed to do more work after the ritual; she was also in my dream with a lot of complex equipment, which I took to indicate that she would be helping me at some point in my process.

As I've read and thought more about this issue, I've realized that there were several points when I probably had experienced soul loss: I have a memory from inside the womb of my mother whining, "But we can't afford to have a baby," and one of being held in her arms as she told someone that sometimes she wished she'd never had me. When I was three, my mother's brother physically forced himself on me and then threatened to kill me if I ever told anyone. When I was nearly twelve, my family was in a head-on collision, the equivalent of hitting a wall going one hundred miles an hour. My father did not survive his injuries and my mother, my brother, and I were never the same; when my father died, my mother gave me emotional responsibility for myself, my brother, and her, and I had no adult to turn to, consult with, or confide in. When I was thirty-three, I left my marriage and my six-year-old son and ten-year-old daughter. Fairly recently, I found out from a relative that as a child I was hit by my mother with some regularity, something I do not remember. A doctor once informed me that my nose had been broken; when I think about the way my mother explained it to me, wondering why no one had ever mentioned it to me before, I have a sense that she may have hit me and broken it.

One more aspect of the issue is this: I have a sense that at whatever age or ages we are when we send a piece or pieces of ourselves away, some part of us remains at that age as we continue through our lives, until some healing takes place and the piece or pieces are restored. For instance, even though my children and I are all adults, when we were together recently and feeling stressed with each other in some small way, I could feel the six-year-old boy in my son and the ten-year-old girl in my daughter. As I thought about it later, I could also sense the nearly twelve-year-old in me and, at moments, even the helpless, unwelcome fetus and infant. If I was not wanted by my true biological creator—my mother—then what possible right could I have to exist, except at her behest, except by pleasing her, and never, ever outshining her? What kind of messages did my children receive from me as they were growing up?

I'm quite sure that each of the events I listed very likely involved some degree of soul loss on my part. And probably coming so close to putting a wonderful life together with my S.O. and then having it come apart was enough to push me over the edge.

The appointment with Serge began with a brief discussion of many of the points I've mentioned above. I was asked why I wanted part or parts of myself back. I was asked why the part or parts would want to come back, what was different now, how is it that it would be safe to come back now, etc. I was asked to name qualities that seem to be lacking in my life; I spoke of creativity, strength, and a feeling of being connected within. Together, we came up with the term "creative self" as the name of the part that would be sought during the ritual.

I was asked to close my eyes, and I was taken through a breathing meditation to a very still place. The journey was recounted as it transpired. My shaman friend took his owl form and then called upon his owl aumakua to assist him. When his aumakua arrived, they set off over the hills and valleys and up into the mountains of an island. At one point, they flew through a fog as dark as night. They continued flying upward until they eventually were above the clouds. Off in the distance rose two razor-sharp peaks with a small valley between them. As they approached the valley, a small village could be seen. Most of the roofs of the buildings were nearly flat and were some soft shade of orange. The aumakua indicated that a particular doorway be entered.

Inside was a large room with a young man of about sixteen, dressed in a robe of mostly orange with a bit of green and red; he was working very intently on a sculpture, with his back to the door. The owl assumed his human form and sent out a tendril of energy to announce his presence. The young man understood that someone had come in, yet he continued to work until he was ready to stop. He then turned with a slight smile—neither happy nor sad. The shaman explained his mission and the reason for his journey. He told the young man what he felt to be the good reasons he might want to consider coming back with him—the things that had changed in my life, ways he would be safer now, and advantages to living a more complete life. He mentioned the young man's energy of creativity, combined with my energy of direction, resulting in directed creativity and creative direction. Afterward, the young man turned back to his work table and began putting his tools into a black wooden box; when they were all put away, he tied the box with a red cloth and slipped it into a slit in the side of his robe. He then indicated that he was ready to leave. For safekeeping, the shaman proceeded to place the young man inside the stone ball he had brought along with him. He then took his owl form once again, left the room, and flew away from the village and down the mountain peaks, retracing the first half of the journey, eventually touching down at an inner place called Bali Hai. The shaman took human form once more and then returned to the room. He gathered the missing part from inside the stone ball and placed it inside me at my navel, sealing the event with a circular motion of his hand.

At the end of this time, my eyes were still closed and there were tears on my cheeks. I opened my eyes and looked around me. There was a noticeable difference in the way I perceived the light around me. I had a feeling not only of seeing differently, but of literally looking through different eyes. I asked if there were any assignments given to follow up something of this nature and was told two things—remember and nurture. Any changes can take hold in a person's life only as they are nurtured over time and allowed to replace old neurological habit patterns. As I was driving back from my shaman friend's house, I noticed the rolling terrain alongside the road. It seemed so different and yet it took me a moment to be able to put words to my experience. Suddenly I realized that I could actually feel what I was looking at. I looked intently at the large trees I was driving by and the same thing was happening. I pulled over to the side of the road to watch the last rays of light strike nearby clouds, and I could feel the color of the golden yellow of the underside and the deep blue-violet of the upper edges. I was entranced and delighted, and wrote a poem before I went to bed.

When I wakened, I looked out at the mango tree just outside my bedroom balcony. As I noticed the colors, the textures, the shape of the trunk and branches, once again I could feel what I was seeing. It is as though I can feel what it's like for aspects of that tree to be that tree, and, if I shift my attention slightly,

I can feel myself as that tree. Both experiences are available to me just by paying a particular quality of attention to what I'm seeing. That night I used a drum to do a bit of journeying and was given the words to a chant: "I am now whole and my faith is restored."

The next night, I used a rattle to journey to the lower world, where I met a white Siberian tiger I had also seen the night before. This time I was suddenly looking at its shoulder up very close and once again I could feel what I was seeing. When I look at my friend's cat, it seems that I can sense what it's like for the cat to be the way it is—for the fur itself to be the color it is, for the muscles to be curved and shaped the way they are, for the eyes to be the color, size, and shape they are, and so on—and this experience seems just to drape over me like a piece of sheer silk, very subtle and very beautiful.

Tonight I was listening to the radio while I was washing dishes, and I wondered if I would be able to hear/feel the music in a manner similar to the way I could see/feel things around me. I began tuning in to the music more closely and, sure enough, I felt the music literally in and around my body. I have been a student of dance and movement meditation for over twenty-five years and have had some profound experiences of movement and sound, yet this sensation was new and more detailed than anything I've ever known. When I turn my attention to the music and just move slightly, I can hear/feel each different instrument, each different voice, each note, each beat—in me and/or around me, moving through me and with me somehow, as though each separate, minute aspect of the experience is a very dear and very close friend.

The night after I finished my first draft of this report, I went upstairs and took a hot bath. As I was about to go to bed, I realized that I needed a glass of water and went down to the refrigerator to get some. As I walked back past the bay window, I noticed that the mama-san chairs next to the window were absolutely bathed in moonlight. Deciding to spend some time exploring this light, I sat down and lay back. The experience was surprising and beautiful. I felt as though I could see pieces of moonlight in the air as I looked up at the moon. I could feel the moonlight touch my skin, and I could touch the moonlight on my moonlit skin. It involved a very subtle physical sensation as well as an emotional one. I began to sing, which I have not felt like doing for quite a while now. I sang "Moonlight Becomes You" and two other romantic songs. It was a lovely and loving exchange between the moon and me.

I'm finishing this report two nights later, after a wonderful experience on a meditative journey. I traveled to the lower world and met my white tiger power animal. I ask him if he would take me to a teacher. He took me upon his back, through woods and up into very high mountains, possibly the Himalayas. We came to an isolated place with a very beautiful small temple, inhabited by one being. As I walked inside, I was struck by the simplicity and the beauty of the huge room, lit only by the sun shining through the most exquisite colors of stained glass. It was literally breathtaking. The man I had been brought to meet invited me to sit or lie down—however I would be most comfortable. At first I felt that I should sit so that I could pay attention to his words better. Waiting for him to speak, I began to feel tremendous energy moving in me. I realized I was receiving a direct transmission from this being and lay down in order to take it in as completely as possible. The feeling was one of an incredible golden and loving light. It fairly sparkled inside me. After a time, I could discern it gradually subsiding. Eventually, I sat up and then stood. The teacher walked me to the door, hugged me warmly, and waved as I returned to my power animal. I was brought back to the starting point of my journey and then came back into the room.

I have spent a certain amount of time in the presence of what I consider to be sacred—psychedelic—plant teacher-beings. What I am experiencing in the few days since this soul-retrieval ritual is in a completely different category. It is much more grounded and feels much more complete, without fragmentation. My awareness of layers upon layers of detail all at the same moment, when I choose to pay attention in this manner, is without precedent in my life. Everything is truly alive and literally waiting to share itself with me. The price of admission to this absolutely beautiful experiential world is simply to turn my attention to something and pause, allowing it to reveal itself and its gifts to me.

I can't say right now what all of these experiences mean or portend, but I'm fairly certain that I have been a person capable of tuning in to these possibilities all of my life. The fact that I felt I needed to send parts of myself away left me diminished to a marked degree, particularly in terms of inner strength and knowing myself. This then left me weakened in certain areas related to the traumas contained within the events themselves; I had great difficulty learning ways of dealing with the parts of life that seemed to come at me, very often out of the blue.

My S.O. once told me about feeling extremely sensitive in many ways as a child. I remember he said that once, when he heard a particular piece of music, he experienced it so powerfully that he felt if he did not do something to temper the effect, he might actually die. When I go over in my mind some of the experiences I've had this week and realize how sensitive I must have been as a very young child, I begin to understand how it was that I sent pieces of myself away, sadly time after time, until I was left literally as a hollow shell of the person I started out to become. I also understand my S.O. as I never could have before.

From my perspective at this moment, I cannot imagine ever feeling anything but love for my S.O. I will love him every moment for the rest of my life and beyond. I bless him for the absolutely integral part he has played in my coming to this place in my life. All of the love and all of the learning I have experienced and continue to experience with him are vitally important in the process of my becoming who I am meant to be.

I want to study and learn more about soul retrieval, until I feel confident to use it in my own work. I believe it to be of great potential value, and I will appreciate the opportunity to share the joy. Isn't it wonderful that shamanism still lives on after all these centuries?

The Novel Description

The following is excerpted from my novel *Dangerous Journey* (Hunaworks, 2002). Lani is a Hawaiian shaman in his early sixties, currently in Germany to help track down an assassin, Nazra, who has esper abilities. Karen is a young Danish esper who has been working with Lani. Karen operates from the second worldview. She has just been tortured by Nazra and is unconscious.

> Lani's soul ached to see the damage that Nazra had done to this kind and beautiful young woman. Clearing those thoughts from his mind, he centered his awareness at his *piko*, his navel, which also served as his meeting point for the center of his being and the center of the universe. He did a special kind of breathing that caused his energy to flow and expand and encompass the woman before him. Using a technique called *ha-ha*, he let his hands move slowly over her entire body about five inches above her skin. This initial series of passes was for gathering information from her energy field about her physical

condition. In addition to the visible bruises that covered nearly every inch of the front portion of her body, with the notable exception of her face, Lani sensed three broken fingers on her right hand, a fractured right collarbone, two fractured ribs on her left side, a fractured tibia on her left leg, and a broken toe on her right foot.

The second series of passes was for increasing the circulation of her blood and activating her lymph system to help relieve muscular and cellular tension, bring more oxygen to assist her own body's repair work and reduce the pain, and start carrying off the toxins built up around the injuries. Lani also spoke to the spirit of her body, as if it were something apart from the spirit of her mind. He used words that would have seemed totally irrational or even insane to someone else if they could have been heard; words like, "I'm glad to see you're healing so quickly. Good thing you're young and strong. In a very short time you'll be looking and feeling good again. Get some more oxygen over there, will you? Relax those muscles, please. Take away those dead red and white blood cells in this area more quickly, okay?"

While part of him dealt directly with the spirit of her body, another part went off in search of the spirit of her mind. This part of her had sought refuge somewhere from the pain and the horror of the experience. If it weren't brought back, there was a chance that Karen might spend the rest of her life in a coma.

This other part of Lani went to a place which has been described as an altered state of consciousness, a dream, another dimension, another world, a figment of imagination, a psychotic state, and other things less kind. Lani would have called it *Po*, a term rather difficult to describe, but which, in its simplest form, could be translated as "a place invisible to outer sight." To Lani's inner perception he was flying in the form of an *'io*, a Hawaiian hawk, over a fantastically shaped and colored mountain range. He was looking for a particular valley that he knew existed, but that he had never been to. A sensation of pulling on his right led him in that direction and soon he swooped over a perfect valley, hidden between a cluster of peaks. He saw perfect waterfalls, perfect trees and flowers, and perfect animals roaming around, mostly of the cat family. In a clearing at the center of the valley was a white, domed temple with a pool nearby and he headed toward it.

On the ground he changed into an ocelot, because he wanted to be exotic without being too large and it was a form he used for other purposes from time to time. He padded up to the temple and looked around, but he didn't see anyone among its alabaster columns. Then he pricked up his ears as a harp cast its notes upon the balmy air and he padded over to the pool. When he arrived there he immediately recognized it as a replica of a Maxfield Parrish painting. The pool and the columns around it had a sort of classical Greek look to them and the whole area, including the lush vegetation around the pool, was bathed in the glowing colors of a fading sunset, even though the valley had seemed to be in morning light when he was flying above it.

A young Adonis in a short, white tunic was seated on a stool at one end of the pool, his fingers producing rich, rippling melodies from a simple lyre that he held on his lap. On the side of the pool opposite Lani-the-ocelot a young Karen, looking to be about fifteen years old, lounged on a padded bench in a long, white robe trimmed in gold. She was eating grapes from a bunch that was held by another young Adonis, twin to the first.

Lani dove into the pool, swam across, pulled himself up on the other side, and shook himself dry. He knew that he didn't really have to shake himself dry, but he liked the sensation. Karen didn't pay any attention to him until he brushed his head against a dangling hand.

"Well, hello there," she said. "My, you're a pretty one. What's your name?"

"Lani," purred Lani.

She didn't act like it was odd that a cat should speak. "Lani . . . ," she said thoughtfully. "That sounds so familiar. But it's a nice name. Do you like the music, Lani?" It was Pachelbel's Canon.

Pretty good for a lyre, thought Lani. "It's beautiful, just like you are," purred Lani.

Karen just smiled and ate another grape.

Lani purred, "I bring greetings from Keoki. And Lisbet. And your landlord, because the rent on your flat in Copenhagen is coming due."

Karen frowned and pushed the grapes away. "You can't talk about things like that in this place."

"Why not? They miss you. Don't you care about them?"

Karen sat up, still frowning. "Stop that! I don't want to go back there to . . . to . . . I just don't want to!" She sighed, relaxed, and looked around. "It's so nice and peaceful here, isn't it? I could stay here forever." She smiled at the Adonis twin and stroked his hand.

"It's very nice," agreed Lani, licking his fur as if he didn't really care what the place looked like. "Your body needs you, though. It's trying to heal itself, but it really needs your help. You could always come back after you've helped it to heal."

The girl looked concerned. "Can't my body get along without me?"

"Not very well," said the ocelot, pacing a bit before sitting back down. "If you don't return to help your body some other people will have to pay for keeping it in a hospital, your landlord will lose money on your lease and will have to sell all your things, your clients will have to find someone less talented to help them, and the man you are going to meet and marry will go unloved. But it's your choice, of course."

She chewed on her lower lip. Adonis One had stopped playing and was just looking at her. Adonis Two had disappeared. "My body . . . hurts," she said finally. "The pain is so terrible . . . I was so helpless . . . why would someone do that to me?" The last was the cry of a very little, bewildered child.

Lani looked intently into her eyes. "Most of the pain is gone, now. No one is there to hurt you anymore. A lot of people are helping you to recover and your body is doing its best to heal itself completely, but it still needs you, and they need you. Besides, like I said, you can come back here and visit any time you want to."

"I can?"

"Any time."

Karen lifted Lani into her lap. Adonis One had disappeared. "How do I go back?" she whispered.

"First, I have to tell you what to do when you do get back," purred the ocelot. "In order to help your body to heal as quickly as possible, you'll have to forgive the person who hurt you and you'll have to forgive your spirit guides for not being able to protect you."

The girl stiffened. "I don't know if I can do that."

"Sure you can, because you're a healer. The best way would be for you to think of that woman as a very lost soul, hurting you only because she is hurting so much. She wasn't attacking you personally, she was attacking everything that had ever hurt her. Can you forgive her for hurting inside so much?"

Karen nodded slowly. "I could forgive her for that."

"Good," said Lani. "Remember that. Now let's talk about your spirit guides . . ."

"Why didn't they protect me!"

The ocelot licked her cheek once. "They're not supposed to protect you from being hurt. That's not their role. They're supposed to protect you from being taken over by negative entities, negative beliefs, and they did that very well. Poor Nazra doesn't have any protective spirits, and so she got taken over. Think about this," Lani purred, "Nazra is an assassin and she didn't kill you when she could have. Perhaps your goodness, and the help of your guides, has helped her just the tiniest little bit." Karen's face brightened at this idea. "So can you forgive your guides for only doing what they were supposed to do?"

"Yes, I can do that, too" said Karen, musingly. "So now what do we do?"

Lani wriggled out of her arms and sat on the bench, looking up at her. "You make yourself very, very small and I'll change into a bird, and then you can ride on my back while I fly us home."

"Oh, that sounds like fun," said Karen, clapping her hands.

Lani turned back into a hawk as Karen shrank to an appropriate size. Then he let her mount his back before spreading his wings and lifting off into the multi-colored sky. He swooped once over the valley so she could get a good look at it from above, and then he took her home.

Back in her body Karen opened her eyes, searched for Lani's hands and found them, and managed a ghost of a smile. "That was fun," she said so softly that only he could hear.

Chapter 10

Magical Flight

O ne of the strangest esper abilities recorded is that of supposedly separating yourself from your physical body and traveling to distant places to see and participate in events otherwise unknown or inaccessible to you, or even floating up to the ceiling and looking down on your body still lying where you left it. Some names for this ability are "magical flight," "astral travel," and "OOBE" (pronounced ooh-bee, meaning "out-of-body experience").

This seems so far outside our normal realm of experience that the tendency is to reject the whole idea as utterly impossible and merely the result of delusions. Before you do that, however, let's talk about it a little more. There is a tremendous amount of misunderstanding in regard to this topic because it is not at all what most people think it is.

First, consider the fact that this concept has been part of the lore of every human society. It is reported to take place among American Indians, including Eskimos, and among East Indians, Brazilians, Mongolians, Polynesians, Japanese,

Chinese, Arabs, Hebrews, Africans, etc. And we shouldn't leave out Europeans and modern American businessmen. From every corner of the globe we get essentially the same story. Certain people, both "ordinary" folks and members of religious or mystical groups (for example, shamans, witch doctors, priests, monks, nuns, and others) "leave" their bodies either spontaneously or by secret methods and travel to Heaven, the Realm of the Gods, or elsewhere; and they "return" with hidden knowledge and tales of wondrous experiences. Or, on a more mundane level, they simply travel around unseen in this physical world, zipping wherever they want to go at the speed of light and passing easily through walls and other obstacles. Sounds like a fairy tale, doesn't it? But another common factor that cannot be disregarded is that, without exception, all those who undergo the experience insist on the *reality* of it. It is no dream, they say. They are aware of what is happening, they have all their cognitive faculties, and the experience is as clear in their memory as any experience in this "outer" world.

Obviously, something is happening here, but what is it? The psychologist is likely to speak of a mental disorder, or at least a hallucination, and possibly recommend the person to a doctor or an institution. He may also look for a history of drug use. It is true that in many cultures, ancient and modern, drugs have been utilized to induce the experience, but there are also a great many reports of people having the experience without drugs. With or without drugs, the psychologist steeped in professional orthodoxy cannot explain where the experiences come from and why they seem so realistic as opposed to other kinds of purely mental activity. To say they are a "product of the mind" is to say nothing at all, and the words *mental disorder* and *hallucination* are only labels used to conveniently hide an uncomfortable subject.

In this chapter, we will explore the hows and whys of this phenomenon, including theories, types of experiences, and, most importantly, the practical benefit of changing reality.

THE OCCULT EXPLANATION

The traditional occult view of the phenomenon of magical flight is quite interesting, though it may sound rather bizarre to those who are not familiar with it. Occultists call the experience "astral projection," meaning the projection of an "astral body" into the "astral plane." It is held that, interspersed with our physical body, there is an astral body made up of a kind of matter vibrating at a much higher frequency than physical matter. This astral body exists partly on this plane and partly on another plane, called the astral. The word *plane* means "dimension," a range of experience outside that of our normal senses. Projection is accomplished by learning various techniques for separating this astral body from the physical one and then willing this astral body to go where and do what one desires. The occult traditions say that this separation is learned only after arduous and dedicated effort stimulated by high spiritual purpose, under the instruction and guidance of a "master" or experienced occultist. This, of course, refers to conscious and voluntary projection. The same occult tradition holds that nearly everyone projects partially or wholly at some time during sleep, and that particularly vivid dreams are memories of this experience.

Unfortunately for the interested layman, the traditional occult system is beset by a complicated dogma. Depending on the particular occult group approached, the person desiring to find out more about this phenomenon will be required to learn all about spirit hierarchies, devas, adepts, masters, guides, rays, a host of bodies (etheric, astral, mental, causal), nature spirits, elementals, negative entities, angels, seraphim and cherubim, the "Dweller on the Threshold," and a huge assortment of other mind-boggling concepts. There is some truth shared through the required education, but it has been so camouflaged that it almost makes one despair at ever finding it. In a time of persecution and ignorance, the dogmatic education may have been necessary, but in a scientifically oriented, fairly well educated, and open society such as we have now, it may be time for a more simple approach to magic flight.

THE SCIENTIFIC EXPLANATION

Although inconsistent in details, the scientific community is fairly well agreed that OOBEs are merely products of the brain, particularly portions of the right hemisphere, due to overstimulation or understimulation of sensory signals, and/or specific electromagnetic stimulation no stronger than that which occurs in our ordinary environment. While quite consistent with the first worldview, the main problem is the paradoxical conclusion that our entire perception of the world around us must be merely the product of our brains, because we perceive the world by electromagnetic stimulation of the brain from all our senses. To say that "certain perceptions are real and other perceptions are not real because we say so" is not scientific.

THE SHAMANIC EXPLANATION

The shamanic explanation is also inconsistent in details among various shamanic cultures, but there is consistent agreement that the shaman can consciously and willfully go out of his body into and through this world and other worlds for the purpose of healing or gaining healing knowledge. These worlds are commonly described as the Upper World, the Middle World, and the Lower World or Underworld. However, some shaman groups go only to one other place, called the Underworld, others think of the Middle World as the one we are in now or a different place, and still others assume a vast multitude of other worlds.

An appropriate question at this point is, What is the difference between a shamanic journey and magical flight?

The correct answer from the shaman's point of view is "none at all." Every one of these worlds is equally real in the shamanic worldview. However, the main focus of this chapter is on going out of your body in this world, which most people do not associate with shaman journeying.

THE EXPERIENCE

The only real way to learn more about magic flight is by direct experience, uncluttered by dogma, and by studying the reports of others who have tried to relate their experiences in a straightforward way. Such reports are few and far between, but they do exist. At Aloha International we have studied the reports, compared them with those of occult and other traditions, and carried out experiments on our own. Though we do not claim to be the last word on the subject, our investigations support the following tentative conclusions:

1. Magical flight/astral projection is as real as any other experience.
2. Our conscious and subconscious minds can and do operate in more than one dimension of experience.
3. The experience is intimately related to telepathic clairvoyance.
4. It is more a case of projecting consciousness than of projecting a body.

5. Bioenergy plays a vital role in the experience.

6. Conscious awareness of the experience is fairly easy to attain, but conscious control is quite difficult.

7. You can learn how to do it.

Before you can learn how to do magic flight, however, you have to learn what we are talking about. In other words, what is the experience like and how do you know you are in it? This is not as easy to discuss as it might seem, because our language is sadly lacking in adequate terms. But let us try.

Several varieties of experience are reported by astral travelers. Attempts have been made by authors to categorize these experiences in spatial terms that serve more to confuse than to explain. Thus, the occult tradition speaks of seven different planes, with each plane having seven subplanes, and the impression is given of a partial interpenetration of one plane with another as they rise up into the sky. One writer, Robert Monroe, uses the terms "Locale I, II, and III," but it is obvious that he doesn't mean they lie in a particular direction. An interesting approach is recorded by John C. Lilly, M.D., in his book *The Center of the Cyclone*. It is an adaptation of an approach used by G. I. Gurdjieff, a Sufi-oriented occultist. Here the experience is described in terms of states of consciousness, ranging from a hell-like state to one of bliss. However, instead of describing an objective state of consciousness, the scale is really only a subjective system for rating one's *reaction* to various states.

One man's hell might be another man's paradise, though they might both be undergoing the same objective experience. Some modern parapsychologists talk about "fields of consciousness." While this has merit, it is so abstract as to be almost meaningless for the average person.

To bring some clarity and comprehensible meaning to this area, I describe the phenomena in terms of types of experience. The following designations are arbitrary. No significance is to be given to the order in which they are listed, as different types might be encountered on different occasions or even during the same occasion.

Type I

This type could be termed the "classic" experience: As far as you can tell, you seem to be in your normal body located right here in the familiar physical world. However, your body seems light as a feather and you may be able to float or fly through the air. You may experience the sensation of leaving your physical body, or you may just suddenly find yourself apart from it. The people around you won't pay any attention to you. They will act as if you don't exist. You may find that you can pass your hand through physical objects (you may or may not feel the texture as you do) and that you can even pass through walls. You may also find that you can will yourself to any physical location you want, more or less. All you have to do is think of the place or a person there, desire to go, and you will be there (although some people feel themselves flying there). The time factor in Type I seems to be the same as in normal consciousness—if you witness an event in this state, you should find, on your return to your body, the event took place at the time you thought it did. On return to your body or during the experience, you might find that what you saw or see is a little distorted from ordinary experience. For instance, if you thought you saw flowered wallpaper in a particular room, you might discover on physical investigation that the wall is actually plain. In the main, though, things will be as you know them to be in ordinary experience.

In a variation of this experience (Type Ia), the people you see may speak to you, but when you question them in a normal state they will not recall having done so. At other times, some people may react fearfully at your presence and later report that they saw a ghostlike apparition. Under some circumstances, you may be able to produce a physical effect on the environment.

Example. I awoke early one morning in my bedroom and immediately noticed that my right arm felt strange. As my awareness increased, I realized that my arm was hanging over the bed and was part way into the floor. I could actually feel the floor covering and the boards and beams underneath. That wasn't pleasant, so I sat up. I saw my wife sleeping to my left and noticed wallpaper on the walls that wasn't there in ordinary life and a dresser across from the bed that we didn't have. When I turned around, I noticed two other things at the same time: a Peruvian rug normally hanging on the wall above the bed had turned into a medieval tapestry, and my normal body was still sleeping, meaning that I was part way in and part way out. I didn't have an inclination to go anywhere, so I lay back down into my physical body and went back to sleep.

Type II

Type II is virtually the same as Type I, but this time you become aware of beings apparently in the same state as yourself. They may or may not be friendly. If they are not, they may try to attack you. As far as we can determine, your fear and/or anger seem only to give them more strength, and it is possible they are only manifestations or projections of your personal suppressed emotions. The best advice I can offer is to remain calm and confident of your ability to see the experience through, for often they will simply dissipate if you don't respond to them, but as a last resort you can always return to the physical. I will explain this later.

Example. During a deep meditation, I suddenly found myself standing in front of a gigantic "King Kong" type of gorilla that was raising its foot to crush me. I felt tremendous fear, but a voice seeming to come from some place inside me said, "Stay calm, just relax and let it happen."

I did that, because it was too late to run anyway, and as soon as the sole of the gorilla's foot touched me, the creature dissipated into nothingness and the fear was gone.

Type III

Type III is similar to Type I in that the surroundings appear normal, but in this case they are unfamiliar and you do interact with the people around you. The culture, social system, and environment may be unlike anything you have ever experienced. It may range from primitive to super-advanced. Some significant characteristics are that you can travel here as in Type I, and you may meet people you know or have known, i.e., those who have "passed over" from the normal world. Whether you accept this or not is up to you. I am only describing what you will experience. Within this type, you may also find areas that correspond to traditional concepts of heaven.

Example. Lani's experience in the previous chapter would fit into this category.

Type IV

If you are familiar with the concept of parallel lives, the fourth type of magical-flight experience appears to be one.

If not, let's just say that it seems to be a world very much like ours that has taken different lines of development, personally, culturally, and/or technologically. This type includes apparent reincarnation experiences, both past and future. It sounds much like Type III, but the difference will be known if you experience it.

Example. Just before I was discharged from the United States Marine Corps, I was confronted with two major choices: to go home to finish my education and marry the woman I loved, or to buy a boat with a friend and sail the South Pacific. Well, in this life I made the best choice and I'm still happily married. Years later I decided to explore the alternate choice in the context of a parallel life and discovered myself dead drunk in a bar in Samoa. Years later I went again and found myself dead. Years after that I went into the same parallel life a few minutes before dying, convinced myself to make some better choices, stopped drinking, and continued with a more productive life in that parallel experience.

Type V

Type V is a weird and often frightening experience because it doesn't relate to anything in normal life. Winds, currents, barriers, darkness . . . word descriptions fail utterly to describe it. It isn't a hell, as such. There are not any tormentors, and there may not be anyone there but you. It is frightening because it seems totally indifferent.

Example. A fairly common experience, shared by myself and others, is either to be floating in a place surrounded by disembodied eyes just staring at you, or to be flying along endless walls made of stone.

Type VI

The sixth type of magical-flight experience could be called Fantasyland, an area of fables, myths, legends, and fairy tales. The impossible can happen here and usually does. In this "place," it seems you are always either helping someone or undergoing a test. Rarely are you ever a simple observer. Perhaps the whole thing is a mental construct for the purpose of self-growth, but it seems very real while you are in it.

Example. A detailed experience of myself living in Atlantis before and after its destruction. Watch for the novel.

Type VII

Type VII reveals a world of light, color, and often sound, with amorphous, flowing shapes. Sometimes there is an awareness of the presence of other beings, always friendly, but they are sensed and not seen. It is extremely pleasant, and you could be quite reluctant to return. This could correspond to the nirvana or samadhi of Oriental religions, or to the union with Christ in the Christian religion. Maybe.

Example. None needed.

Type VIII

Call this type of magical-flight experience *hell,* for lack of a better word. No other description is needed. It is rarely encountered by those who have prepared themselves for an out-of-body experience.

Example. Forget it.

Types IX, X, XI, etc.

These types signify a dual-consciousness effect. It is possible to be totally unaware of your physical body and surroundings during the above experiences, or to be aware of existing in both states at the same time. Again, words are inadequate. It must be experienced to be understood or, rather, appreciated.

Example. A time when I was fully awake and aware while lying in bed and fully awake and aware while walking along some cliffs in another place.

There you have it. No wonder the unprepared crack up and the uninformed want to put away the ones who do report it. Yet there is such a reality about these experiences that they should be explored by as many clear-minded and adventurous people as possible so we can learn what all the possibilities are. If we can develop the skill of using them to change the reality in which you are reading this book, our whole way of living is in for a sharp revision.

METHODS

For those who haven't been frightened away so far, I will now present some of the basic methods to initiate an out-of-body experience. We are concerned here with as much conscious control over the experience as possible, so I will not discuss spontaneous experiences or the use of drugs, alcohol, or deep hypnosis guided by someone else.

The Dream Method

One of the more common methods worldwide, this one consists of establishing control while in the midst of a dream.

To do so, you must become aware that you are dreaming. This kind of experience is usually called "lucid dreaming," and it can happen spontaneously or on purpose. Then you can use your will to take charge and direct the experience. However, this is easier to say than to do.

First, you must pay more attention to your dreams, especially ones in which you are using your critical faculties. For instance, suppose you dream you are riding a unicorn, but at the same time you are thinking to yourself in the dream, "This is crazy, there's no such thing as a unicorn!" At this point, you are in the right state to turn the dream into a magical flight, but you must become aware of this fact during the dream. Then you focus your attention on an object in the dream landscape until it wavers and changes (an alternative is to focus on your hands). If you have been able to maintain conscious awareness up to this point, you can now decide to go where you want and you will be there.

Before you go to sleep, strong suggestions to have such an experience will be of great help. However, making such a suggestion after you wake up in the morning and purposely going back to sleep gets even better results. Some people claim that eating fish or cheese for dinner increases the possibility, or putting a pinch of salt on your tongue as well. I have had inconsistent results with those approaches.

It may take weeks, months, or years to get good results, but many people have had success with the dream method.

The Picture Meditation Method

This method utilizes either a physical picture or a mental one. In either case, you use your imagination to make the picture seem as real as possible, including input from all five senses. Then you imagine yourself in the picture, not an image of you, but *you*, as if you were really there taking in all the sights, sounds, and sensations. If you visualize well enough and practice regularly, you will be there in an astral projection, perhaps only for a few seconds at first, but eventually as a complete and vivid experience. A related alternative is the Memory Method, in which you create a vivid memory recall of a person or place instead of using a picture. I have had a great deal of success with both of these methods.

The Repetitive Route Method

This method may sound dull, but it has its adherents and its record of successes. To apply it, choose a short route between two points in a place where you will be undisturbed. Let's say you choose a route from your bedroom to the bathroom. Along the way you tape four or five markers at various spots in order to fix these points in your mind. First you lie down on your bed, then you get up and move physically to each of your markers, spending several minutes at each to strongly imprint the point in your memory. On your return from the bathroom, you do the same thing. Repeat this procedure five times. Then lie on the bed and cover the same route in your imagination, being sure to spend the same amount of time as you did physically. Do this five times as well. Repeat the whole thing in the physical and again in the imagination. That's all for the first session. Do the entire practice once a day until you find yourself returning from the bathroom in what you thought was a physical trip and see your body still lying on the bed. Try not to get shaken up. Isn't this what you wanted?

The Partner Method

This requires a friend who can guide you into a relaxed state and give you the suggestions necessary to get you started. Deep hypnosis is *not* the object. All you need are some suggestions to relax and a few more to the effect that you are moving your consciousness out of your body to some predetermined point. Then you take over completely. The suggestions by your partner shouldn't take longer than five or ten minutes. As an alternative, you can record your own voice on tape and preset the amount of time you want to spend in the experience. I use variations of this in some of my workshops with very good results.

The Symbol Method

This method has numerous variations found all over the world. Essentially, it consists of staring at a symbol for a minute or more, or until you can look away and see a clear complementary image. Then you close your eyes, retain the image, and visualize it growing large enough to step through, which you do in your mind. If you are relaxed and ready for it, this will be the jumping-off point for an astral trip. You can use religious symbols, occult symbols, geometric figures, I Ching hexagrams, or anything that strikes your fancy. A good alternative is to imagine the symbol on a door, make the door as real as you can, and then open it and walk through.

The Isolation Method

This method involves reducing your physical sensory input as much as possible *without* going to sleep. The result is often an out-of-body experience (or hallucination, depending on who you describe it to). It's a favorite method in some shamanic cultures, where the apprentice may be wrapped in a blanket and left in an underground hole or cave for several days, or sent into a lonely wilderness without any food or human contact for several days. This type of vision quest may result in an experience of magical flight. In ancient Hawaii, the same effect could be achieved by sailing alone to a small and distant island.

There are many ways to do this in our modern cultures; it depends on individual susceptibility. For some people it takes only a couple of hours in a bare room with nothing to do. Sitting or lying in a dark room or closet will do for others. Isolation tanks work well for this, as do meditation techniques in which you are supposed to make your mind a blank. Narrowing your attention to one sensory input will also work; for example, by staring at a single object (still or moving), listening to one monotonous sound, focusing on the touch of one thing, and doing one or another of these either physically or mentally. These actions work because your conscious mind needs active stimulation to stay focused, and if it doesn't get it in this world, it will hop over to another one.

The Spinning Method

Used by Celtic druids and, later, witches and wizards in Europe, this is a technique of sensory overload, which produces the same results as the isolation method above, because if the conscious mind has too much input, it will sometimes shift its focus into another state. One way of achieving this in earlier times was for the practitioner to suspend him- or herself in a hanging cage and have an assistant spin the cage around and swing it at the same time. In a curious Kauai story recorded by Martha Beckwith in *Hawaiian Mythology*, the shamanic archetype Maui goes to visit his father in the Pleiades. Hidden meanings in place and object names are common in Hawaiian, and it may be significant that two names associated with this journey both contain the concept of spinning in their roots.

The Counting Method

I use this method when I am teaching time travel because it is very helpful in keeping the focus mind focused during past, future, and parallel life experiences. It has a superficial resemblance to hypnosis because of the counting, but there is no trance induction involved and it can be done with or without a helper. The method, as outlined below, assumes a shift of consciousness to a past life.

1. Take a deep breath and close your eyes. Think of a past time period you would like to visit, or a past role or skill that you want to explore.
2. On a backward count of ten you will go to that past life. Ten . . . one . . . be there.
3. Are you wearing anything on your feet? Move up. Are your legs bare or covered? Move up. Are you male or female? Move up. What kind of clothing do you have on? Move up. What kind of hair do you have? Are you wearing any jewelry or decorations? Are you inside or outside? Are there any other people around? What do you do for a living? (Plus any other questions you want to ask.)

4. On a backward count of five you will move to the happiest time of your childhood in that life. Five . . . one . . . be there. What is happening now?

5. On a forward count of five you will move to your time of greatest skill in that life. One . . . five . . . be there. What is happening now?

6. On a forward count of ten you will go forward to your current life and remember anything you can make use of from the past life to help your current life. One . . . ten . . . be *here*. Move your fingers and toes, take a deep breath, and remember what you learned.

For a parallel life, you would move back to a point in your life when you had to make a major choice between two or more decisions. The assumption here is that a parallel life was generated for each major choice that you did not make.

The Alternate-Body Method

The alternate-body method is one of my favorites and the one I teach most in my courses. It consists of creating an exteriorized thoughtform of something suitable in front of you and then transferring your conscious awareness into it. I generally make an animal, but any kind of being or vehicle would work. I demonstrate this in workshops by going somewhere out of sight, energizing myself, creating the thoughtform, moving my awareness into it so that I see out of its eyes, sense through its senses, and move with its muscles. This takes me a couple of minutes, at most. Inside the thoughtform vehicle, I then go into the classroom, touch a few people, make a lot of noise, do something outrageous, and return to my body. Next, I walk back into the classroom and ask everyone what they saw, felt, heard, or thought about. Invariably, a few will have seen what form I took and what I did. Others will have picked up portions of it, some will have noticed the air looking "funny" in different places, some will have felt touch or movement, and a few will not have experienced anything out of the ordinary. After that, I teach them how to create a thoughtform and have them move into that form and go to another room, where I have placed an object on the floor. They are supposed to look at it through the eyes of the form and come back and report. Finally, we all walk into the room to look at the object with our normal eyes. A few will have seen it exactly through their form, most will have seen portions of it or symbols of it, and a few will have gotten distracted by something else. I like this method best because it is fast and simple.

HOW OTHERS PERCEIVE YOU

The last method brings up an important point to consider— how others may perceive you while you are in a state of magical flight. Here some typical experiences others may have of you:

- *Spontaneous Attention.* Some people report that their attention was suddenly drawn to a certain area in their environment without knowing why and without seeing anything in particular. This effect has been tested in cases in which it was known that a magical flyer was in that location at that time.
- *Funny Air.* Some people notice a sort of concentrated shimmering in the air, like a small area of heat waves, only thicker.
- *Ghost.* Some see a ghost-like form, usually human-shaped.
- *Energy Body.* Some see a sparkling outline of a human body.
- *Translucent.* Some see a human form that is not quite solid.
- *Semi-Solid.* The form appears solid, but does not feel right if touched. At this stage, people may be able to hear you speak.
- *Solid.* The form looks and feels like a real person, able to speak and make physical contact. As a side note, the more solid the flyer seems, the less solid the original body will seem.

You may have noticed the progression above, from virtually nothing to solid. The primary factor involved is the degree of focus held by the flyer, but the flyer's level of energy and the perceiver's mind/body state are additional factors that may influence the perception.

PURPOSE

So far all this magical flying sounds like entertainment, even if it's valid. Why bother? Let me remind you that the whole purpose of this book is to teach you various ways of changing reality. Magical flight may be one of the more subtle ways, but it can have great effects. Unlike journeys, which change this reality by changing symbols of this reality, magical flight changes reality mostly by influencing *people* to change. What follows are some practical applications.

Helping Others

There are many ways to help people during magical flight.

Attracting or Distracting Attention
Sometimes you can influence a person's attention at a critical moment that can help them move toward a healthier, more positive, or safer situation.

Positive Suggestions
While you can always send telepathic suggestions, the greater energy level and proximity of magical flight can help make those suggestions more influential. Just as in the first worldview, however, a person is no more likely to follow a suggestion from someone in magical flight than they

are to follow a suggestion given face to face, unless the suggestion matches the person's motivation.

Energetic Assistance

Following the precepts of telekinesis, you can add your energy to something someone else is doing physically to make what they are doing more effective. This technique has been used to help people in the water stay afloat longer, help them lift things when necessary, and even help them heal someone.

Guidance and Direction

Apart from giving telepathic help during magical flight, if you can achieve at least the semi-solid state, you can act as a very realistic and present helpful stranger. There are many stories of people who have received direct help from a mysterious stranger who then walked out of sight and disappeared. At least some of these instances are cases of getting help from someone who is using magical flight. My most dramatic use of this to date took place many years ago when I learned that a family of five had become lost in the jungles of the Central African Republic. First I magically flew to the area and located the family. Then I located a road-construction crew not too far away. Finally I appeared to the family in the semi-solid form of a local guide and led them to the construction site. As they rushed forward to the workers, I stepped back into the jungle and faded back into my normal body.

Direct Physical Influence

While this is possible for the flyer who can achieve a solid form, it generally takes a tremendous amount of energy, concentration, and motivation to sustain this state for more than a few moments while also maintaining your original body at its location. Still, there are times when you might be able to offer critical help to someone by being able to move something during magical flight. Plan on a great amount of practice in order to do it, however.

Helping Yourself

There are several ways in which magical flight can help you to help yourself.

Concentration Training

Magical flight requires the development of a high degree of concentration ability, an ability that will be of great benefit in all the other ways of changing reality.

Information Gathering

You can learn to fly in your magical body to many places to get important information that you can use in other methods of reality changing. Don't expect anything like one hundred percent accuracy in your perception of these places, though (see Troubleshooting, below). Sometimes the "feel" of a place can be more accurate and more useful than the physical layout. One time when I was hiking in the mountains of California and heading toward a place called Rattlesnake Canyon, I magically flew through the canyon before I got there physically, to check on where the snakes might be. I didn't see any snakes during my flight, but I got a strong "feel" of snakes. Back in my body, I rolled pink fog through the valley and broadcast a telepathic message to any snakes listening that I was only passing through and meant no harm. During my hike through the valley, I saw several snakes quietly curled up several yards/meters off the path. On other occasions, I have used magical flight to check on the weather at a destination. They I've come back to my body and used telepathic influence to stop the rain for my arrival.

Healing Yourself
When you engage in magical flight, you are moving your consciousness from one dream to another related dream, because the only dreams you can move to are those somehow related to the dream of your daily life. And, since changing one dream changes all related dreams, you can use your conscious will to change the story, just as you would for a night dream, and reap the healing benefits in ordinary, present-moment reality. I have used this method with considerable success by working with the past and the future.

Developing Yourself
Please bear with me—this isn't easy to explain and it has to do with parallel lives. I've mentioned the idea that parallel

lives are generated at points of major decisions, in fulfillment of the "unmade" choice. Although they are called "parallel," these lives do not really run parallel like streets. If you wanted to make a two-dimensional diagram to represent them, it would look more like goat tracks that cross over each other more or less frequently. The crossover points are places where the two lives meet energetically and can be times of high creativity for both lives. As an example, there was a time in my life when I felt I had to make a big decision between being a writer (which included public speaking) and an artist (which included music, painting, and sculpture). Before I learned about how parallel lives really work, all I knew was that sometimes I would get these odd impulses to make things, draw pictures, or play music. After I found out about parallel lives, I learned that I could use those impulse times to merge my writer dream self with my artist dream self and experience a great burst of energy and creativity. The way I began was to actually make something (like a simple shelf or model boat), draw or paint something (usually on my computer), or play my ukulele. Doing these things gave me a great feeling of personal satisfaction that spilled over into my "normal" life. I felt at times like I was painting with written words and sculpting with spoken words, and I could write poetry and songs that would enhance what I did as a writer. By using magical flight, I also learned useful things from my artist's life, as well as the interesting information that at these times he wrote articles and gave lectures about his art.

CHAPTER 10

Troubleshooting

Weird things can happen during magical flight, and this section will help you deal with them.

False Fears

One of the greatest fears promoted by those who should know better is the fear that you won't be able to get back into your body. Don't believe any of the tales that claim this has happened to someone. It's just as false as what we call today an "urban legend." You will always be able to get back in your body, because your consciousness is the only thing that left it. Any astral body that you've generated for your flight is only a temporary energy construct that will dissipate when you return your focus to your physical body.

The second greatest fear is based on an occult assumption that everyone remains attached to their physical body by a silver cord when they astral travel, and, if that cord ever gets severed, you die. Personally, I have never seen such a cord, but I know that if you expect one strongly enough you can generate it. Again, if it appears, it's only an energy construct that will dissipate when you return you focus to your physical body.

Distortion

I have mentioned this phenomenon more than once, so I will explain it more clearly here. Every dream has what we can call a "frequency pattern" that is different from

246

every other dream. My dream of life is different from your dream of life, even if we share the same assumptions, and what I experience will be slightly or radically different from what you experience, even in the same location.

Let's call our everyday reality, regardless of which worldview we use, Life Prime, and imagine it for the moment as a sheet of paper. When we travel with our consciousness in magical flight, we are moving into a different range of frequencies that may differ more or less from our normal range of focus. Let's call that Life One. Life One would be a slight variation of Life Prime, and we can imagine it as a second sheet of paper lying right on top of the first one. They are very close to each other, but not exactly the same. The room I woke up in during my nonflying magical flight in my bedroom could be called Life One. What I saw was basically the same bedroom I was used to, except for the wallpaper, the dresser, and the tapestry. And my semi-separation from my physical body, of course. The closer we are to the frequency pattern of Life Prime while in magical flight, the more similar it will be, but it will never be the same. That's why it can't be used with any accuracy for spying. The farther away from Life Prime you get, like the top of a ream of paper, the more unlike Life Prime your experience will be.

Distraction

Holding your concentration during magical flight is a challenge. Sometimes the slightest thought, association, or stimulation can send you whizzing away to a completely different sheet of paper. I will illustrate this with another excerpt from *Dangerous Journeys*, based on an actual experience of mine but much better described in the story. Again, to set the scene, Keoki is a young Hawaiian, apprenticed to his grandfather for shaman training. He is on a train in Germany.

> Keoki settled back and used the special breathing that got him deeply centered. While in that state he decided to explore the train.
>
> He sent his awareness forward through the next two cars to the engine. He was careful not to try and pay attention to details. Gramps had told him that *Po*, the inner world, was like a stack of photographs of different places, with each photo being like a different layer, or zone, of experience. It was difficult to keep your focus in one zone without slipping over into another zone, perhaps many layers away. The trick to staying in one zone was to keep your focus moving within a certain range of experience related to the zone you wanted to stay in. Gramps had said that the same thing applied to *Ao*, the outer world, but Keoki hadn't really understood until he read somewhere that fighter pilots had to be wary of focusing too intently on a single target or they would go into a trance.
>
> So Keoki let his consciousness drift along within the range of the train experience, no more than a few layers away from *Ao*. At the engine he let himself feel the electricity pouring into the engine itself and followed its transformation into the mechanical movement that

drove the wheels. When he tired of that he drifted back, through his own car and over his own body, into the dining car. He observed how it was set up and made a mental note to check his perceptions when he got back to his body. He kept moving, into the second class cars, until he came to the bicycle car.

He was riding a red velvet bicycle along the narrow ridge of a purple mountain range that crossed the center of an island from sea to golden sea. The air was filled with rose petals that kept obscuring his vision, and he was afraid he would ride straight off the edge of the ridge. He batted them away with one hand, causing his bike to wobble dangerously. The bicycle told him to stop that before the ogre-dance caused a mass rift in the circular plenifold and . . .

The bicycle told him what? What was he doing on a bicycle anyway? He remembered something Gramps had said: If you're ever lost in inner space, return right away to your body. Keoki willed himself back and woke up in his compartment on the train to Freiburg. He looked around, moved his hands and feet, touched the seat cushion, and stood up. Now he knew what had happened. He had been caught by an *aka* thread connecting the bicycles of the layer he'd been in to another *aupuni po*, another inner realm, so fast he didn't notice it. He knew what had happened, but he didn't understand it. *Po* was a complicated place.

I think that's all you need to know for now. May you always fly fast, fly far, and fly well.

Chapter 11

Purple Feathers

$\sim$

In one of my courses in Hawaii called HunaQuest, I emphasized the flexible nature of reality. During one of these courses, given on Kauai, we ended up on the beach at Hanalei Bay, under tall ironwood trees that moved gently in the soft sea breeze; we gathered in a passive kind of meditation known as *nalu*. The exercise required that people pick something fairly unusual to meditate on. The object of our focus, chosen at random from the group of fourteen people, was a purple feather. That is, we each conjured up a feeling/image of a purple feather in our minds and held that concept in our awareness without judgment or expectation for several minutes. And that was it.

The purpose was to see whether and how a purple feather might appear in someone's experience over the next few days. I told the class that they might see an actual one, a picture of one, or they might just read or hear about one. Then we dropped the matter and went on to something else.

BREAKING ALL THE RULES

The first time I came across this kind of experiment was in Richard Bach's book *Illusions*, where the object to focus on was a blue rose. At the time, in the seventies, I did the focus not expecting much from it. The next day my first client at my office in Marina del Rey came in wearing a dress with blue roses on it. It also happened to be my mother's birthday, and when she came in to visit me that afternoon I gave her a birthday card with red roses on it. Then, without knowing anything about my focus experiment, she mentioned that my father had always given her a blue rose on her birthday, something I had never heard her say before.

Now, I was already quite familiar with ideas about the possibility of changing reality from Huna, Hawaiian shamanism, and other studies, but it's one thing to know it as a theory or even a gradual process and quite another to experience it so directly, so quickly, and so simply.

Of course, the first reaction from most people would be to call what I've described a coincidence. What possible connection could there be between a simple, unemotional thought and an experience in the outside world? Well, one time could be coincidence; two times maybe; three times possibly. But how about a hundred times? Over the years I've done this experiment myself and with others well over a hundred times with the same result. Think of something, anything, clearly and with a minimum of tension, and it will appear in your environment within three days to a week, in some form or another.

That last part is significant. "In some form or another" means that your thought doesn't necessarily appear as an object. In fact, the way in which it appears may be quite varied. It could be an object, or a picture, or a drawing, or you could read about it, or you could hear someone talking about it. Yes, I know the objection: you might just be noticing something that might be around anyway. But remember the number of times this has happened consistently and consider that the experiments have involved purposely unusual objects.

I am not necessarily saying that the thoughts bring the experiences into existence. That's only one theory of how it could happen. Perhaps we are shifted into an alternate reality where the experiences exist. Or maybe our thoughts merely attract existing experiences to us, or us to them. At this point it doesn't really matter. There are many possible explanations, but coincidence isn't one of them. The main point is that reality isn't what we've been taught it is. Reality isn't just "out there," something separate from what we think and feel. There's an intimate connection between "in here" and "out there." One of the greatest adventures of life is exploring that connection.

But back to the purple feathers. The first result of our beach meditation came the night of the experiment, when the class was having dinner together. It really wasn't much. One of the students sitting next to me showed me a piece of an orchid that had fallen from her lei having the color and shape of a purple feather. The next result came the next day when my colleague Susan went to dinner with her mother at the Marriott Hotel. As she told me, when they reached the bottom of the escalator taking them down to the lobby she noticed that two *kahili,* or feather standards formerly used by Hawaiian royalty, which stood on each side of the escalator were made of purple feathers—not typical of the ones used during the monarchy. Then it began to get much more interesting. A student from Paris reported: "Just to let you know that on Saturday after our last day of the HunaQuest, I noticed that the fabric of the bedspreads in my hotel room had a design with purple feathers in it—I think this counts!" A student from Germany wrote: "We had a good journey back home to Germany, and in my apartment on Monday I found a purple feather on the floor." And the student from Paris added: "My daughter and I both collect feathers. She arrived back in Paris from the U.S. on Monday and, with no knowledge of our purple feather story, presented me with a purple feather as a gift." By Tuesday, a little longer than three days, all the students of that class had been told about the purple-feather findings of the others, and so everyone had a purple feather experience of some kind.

NOT JUST FEATHERS

During another class we picked Pegasus, and winged horses popped up all over the place. In a European class we picked a green cat, and the ways in which green cats, and all kinds of cats, appeared were amazing, and this was only during the lunch break. Some students and I saw a cat run into a bush, and the people who lived there said they hardly ever saw cats running loose. One student gave me a green glass cat that she noticed in a store window, and another student brought back a book that a friend had just given her that day featuring a painting of a green cat by a famous artist. And on and on it goes.

Were the purple feathers and Pegasus horses and cats already there in our environment? Quite possibly. But something we did with our minds brought them from somewhere into our awareness and experience. After all, seeing blue roses and receiving purple feathers and green cats as gifts are not everyday occurrences. So it isn't as if all these things were just there and we didn't notice them, although a lot of first-level thinkers would prefer it that way.

Believe in coincidence if you like, but I think you'll get more out of life if you pay extra attention to the relationship between your thoughts and your experience. It just might give you an edge on making your dreams come true. As another student put it after hearing about all the purple feather experiences, "What a great lesson in awareness and being in the moment. It made me realize that sometimes when I am intensely preoccupied, I wouldn't notice a purple feather (or whatever else I might need) if it dropped down and draped itself around me."

PROGRAMMING THE DREAM

An American metaphysical idiom you will often hear is, "Let's program for something good to happen." The general meaning of this is to use a combination of words, imagery, and positive emotion to bring about a desired event. Most of the people who use this kind of phrase have no idea that it derives from the concepts used in modern computer programming.

To "program" a computer means to insert into the computer's memory a sequence of coded symbols that will enable or induce the computer to perform a desired function that is different from what it can do with its built-in instructions. In computer language, the built-in instructions are called "firmware" and the added instructions are called "software." The native language of the computer is composed of ones and zeros only, but if the software is well written it can translate the coded symbols into its own language and produce the desired results. Usually. Or at least, more often than not.

Computer programming provides a good metaphor for what we can do with our minds and bodies. The focus mind provides the software (word and image symbols) and the body provides the hardware (memory and expectations) plus energy. When the mental software is well presented (it matches what the body mind believes is possible), then the biocomputer outputs the signal into the world dream and something changes.

Passive Programming

As demonstrated in the purple feather experiment, changing reality does not require much energy as long as the symbols used do not evoke any fear or doubt (in computer terms, they do not conflict with existing programs). In the class, we avoided that problem by focusing in a very passive way on an unusual image not related to any significant goal or purpose. The exercise can also be done in a passive way with a definite purpose in mind. Here are some examples of that type of programming.

The Wall
In an early experiment with magical flight I sat in a meditative position facing a wall that was between me and another room. For an extended period of time I passively imagined myself sitting in the same position, facing in the same direction, on the other side of the wall. At one point I was suddenly there, on the other side, looking around at that room, and then a few moments later I was back in my original location. There was no sense of transition in either direction, and my feeling was that I was actually there. I acknowledge that it may have been magical flight, but it felt like my whole self had moved.

The Impossible Itinerary
At the beginning of a long and complicated trip to Europe, my wife and I arrived at the ticket desk in Honolulu to

discover that our whole itinerary had disappeared from the airline computer system. We both stayed perfectly calm and vocally thanked and complimented the ticket agent for every small positive thing she did, at the same time ignoring everything that did not seem to work out. Inwardly, we passively, but consistently, blessed with images and silent words all the personnel involved, all the computers and electrical connections, all the planes that might be part of our trip, and everything good we could think of. The agent went more and more out of her way to help us, and so did the people she was dealing with. In about an hour we had a better itinerary than our original one—with first-class seats thrown in as a bonus.

Flossie the Flop
For several days, Hurricane Flossie made international news and was featured more than once on CNN. She slowly headed toward the southern part of the Big Island, and there was near panic in the community. As she got closer, schools and many businesses all over the island were closed, coastal roads and beach access paths were closed, and the National Weather Service put out flash flood warnings and watches. Even when it was clear that Flossie was going to pass south of the island, all measures stayed in effect, and it was officially expected that high winds, very heavy surf, and very heavy rains would hit us as she passed. While all this was going on, a great many friends on and off the island were passively programming that Flossie would

keep going farther south and would rapidly diminish in strength without doing any damage. We all used different symbols in our programming. Mine was of the posted tracking image, which I modified in accordance with our plan. During the time that Flossie was passing south of us, my immediate area had only very light, occasional drizzle with no wind. Hilo, which was expected to get ten to fifteen inches (twenty-five to thirty-five cm) of rain, got only two inches (five cm). The high winds were only fairly strong gusts along the coast, and the surf never got higher than what most of our tropical storms produce.

Of course, you may rightly question whether our mental programming had anything to do with the behavior of the hurricane, but consider this: not only did the storm do exactly what we wanted it to do against all expectations, but we had done similar things against all expectations many times before, so we had a success memory behind our efforts. Of course it doesn't always work exactly, because the storm or whatever may have its own agenda, but there is always a lessening of the problem.

Active Programming

Sometimes, instead of passive programming, the only thing that will make a change is active programming, meaning highly focused intention combined with strong emotional energy. This works very well when there is a large amount of doubt and also when there is a small amount of fear. If there is a lot of fear plus a lot of related success memories, energetic programming can still work. However, if there is a lot of fear and practically no related success memories, energetic programming may cause a backlash that will make things worse. There is a solution to that, but the best way to understand the information in this paragraph is through examples.

The Missing Briefcase

After doing a workshop in Los Angeles, I arrived home to discover that I was missing my very nice Samsonite brief-case with my workshop materials in it, so I naturally called the hotel venue. They sent someone around to the work-shop room and the lost and found and reported that there was no sign of my briefcase. When I hung up the phone, I was just about to give up and assume someone had taken it. Then I suddenly decided I wasn't going to accept that. If reality really was as flexible as a dream, as I taught, then I should be able to remanifest my briefcase. I worked myself up to a near-angry emotional state and demanded that the Universe bring my briefcase back. While I was still pacing back and forth, ranting and raving, the phone rang and someone from the hotel said they had found my brief-case. Happy at the news and proud of my success, I rushed back to the hotel. There, I was told that no one had called me and my briefcase still wasn't there. I returned home dumb-founded. What was that all about? Nevertheless, I decided that I still wasn't going to give up. Again, I did some very energetic programming, but nothing more happened that day. The next day, though, I got another call saying that my briefcase had been found and I could come and get it. Pleased but cautious, I returned once more to the hotel, and once more they said no one had called. This time I insisted that the janitor take me to all the possible places my briefcase could be, but we didn't find it. On my way out of the hotel, escorted by the janitor, my attention was suddenly attracted to a closed, dark office with windows onto the hallway. For some reason, I was moved to walk over and look in the window, even though the janitor was telling me it was the manager's office, that he had been gone for two weeks, and that his office was locked and no one was supposed to go in it. And yet, sitting next to the manager's desk was my briefcase. It took quite a bit of persuading to get the janitor to open the office, but when he did I was able to prove that the briefcase was mine, and it is still mine thirty-some years later. The real mystery is this: who called me twice?

The Texas Conundrum
After a workshop on Kauai, one of the students from Texas stopped over in Honolulu on the way home and found that he had left two Hawaiian shirts back on Kauai. Inspired by my briefcase story, he energetically programmed for them to appear in his hotel room, but it didn't happen, so he gave up on the shirts and on my dream theories. Back in Texas, he arrived at the home he shared with his daughter, carried

his bags directly from his car to his bedroom, and began unpacking. A few minutes later his daughter, who had stayed in Texas the whole time, came to his room from hers, holding two tightly-bunched wads of clothing. "Where did these come from, Dad?" she asked. They were the two shirts he had left on Kauai.

The two stories above illustrate a phenomenon that often occurs with energetic programming: when you are success-ful at remanifesting something, it doesn't always appear where you expect it to. The probable reason is that there must be a great many variables we don't know about yet.

The Toothpaste Cap

On a workshop tour in Denmark, I stayed for a few days in a small cottage on a country estate. The sink in the bathroom was normal in every respect, except that the sink drain emptied into a pipe that ended about a foot (thirty cm) above a floor drain. While I brushed my teeth one morning, the cap on my toothpaste tube slipped out of my fingers and then went into the sink drain and through the short pipe. As I backed up and watched it go into the floor drain, I thought of all the inconvenience that would cause and shouted, NO! with a great deal of energy. The next moment, I actually saw the cap rematerialize beside the drain it had just gone into. Although a relatively insig-nificant event, it represents the only visual experience of rematerialization I have ever had.

An additional curious phenomenon in this area is the rarity of visually witnessing rematerialization. Most of the time it happens out of sight. I suspect to the reason is our habitual patterns of belief and expectation that inhibit such awareness.

MALLEABLE MATTER

We can change the material world in strange and wondrous ways, because the material world changes itself in strange and wondrous ways without our intervention.

This should not be surprising, since we find evidence for it in all four worldviews. The Objective Level tells us that all matter is in a state of constant change, that what seems to be solid matter is actually mostly space, and that what little matter there is in that space is mostly composed of electrical charges and waves. The Subjective Level tells us that everything is energy, that everything is connected, and that mental energy changes emotional energy, which changes physical energy. The Symbolic Level says that everything is a dream symbol and that, when one symbol changes, all related symbols change. The Holistic Level says that everything is one and that when one thing changes, all things change. It is important to note that, while this book is concentrating on consciously directed change, the various worldviews assume that change can happen regardless of our conscious involvement.

Rather than being a digression, this section is intended to increase our awareness of natural change, especially the strange and wondrous. The very fact that such things happen naturally may stimulate us to find out how to make them happen consciously. After all, we fly in airplanes because birds fly, we live in houses because animals build nests and shelters, we grow crops because it's more efficient than gathering wild plants, and we smelt iron because lava melts rocks. Everything we do today to change our environment and our lives had its origin in observations of natural change and influence.

Stories of Wondrous Change

In keeping with my established format, I am going to use personal experiences for examples of the strange and wondrous.

Time Dilation/Contraction

I have had many experiences when time has not changed in its expected second-by-second, minute-by-minute, hour-by-hour pattern, and so have many of my students from all around the world. One of the most common experiences of this type is when you need to be somewhere and you know you won't make it because of how long it takes to get there, and, in spite of that, you arrive on time or early. Less common, but still frequent, is when you know how long something will take and it takes much longer without any apparent reason.

Subjective perception is undoubtedly a factor in some of these cases. On a trip to Bora Bora, a group of friends and I purposely made a pact to maintain a present-moment focus during a three-day stay, and our joint memory is that it felt like we were there for seven days. On the other side, it is well known that the more you don't want to be where you are, the more it feels like time is passing slowly. And the more you are enjoying yourself in a narrow focus, intellectually or emotionally, the faster time seems to go.

This is not what I mean, however; I'm talking about times when, by the clock, an airplane trip or a car trip or a hike take less time than seems possible, or even longer than seems possible.

We measure the passage of time by quantifying the interval between two events in space as we perceive it. The nature of time, therefore, is dependent both on our perception and on the nature of space. If distances in space are not constant (see below) and if our perception is not constant (no surprise there), then obviously time cannot be constant.

Here is an experiment with time that you can perform, by yourself or with a group. It doesn't prove anything, but it is strange.

1. Place a large clock where you can see it clearly. A clock with a smoothly sweeping second hand is best, but even one that jumps at one-second intervals will do.

2. Close your eyes and imagine an object or a scene. I don't know why, but imagining something neutral produces a more pronounced effect than something interesting or emotional.
3. After fifteen seconds or so, quickly open your eyes and look at the second hand. For most people, the second hand will stand still for longer than it should before moving again. And that means, for you at least, that time has actually stopped for a moment.

Teleportation

Teleportation refers to moving an object instantly from one location to another location without any travel in between. It is seen mostly in *Star Trek* episodes, video games, and virtual worlds, but it does occur in Life Prime. I have never met anyone who could (or would) demonstrate this as a conscious skill, but in every workshop I have given that included this topic, there have always been a good percentage of students who have experienced the spontaneous form. Below are two of my experiences, both of which took place in vehicles.

1. *Ten Miles in No Time.* I was seventeen, driving home late at night from a date with the woman who was eventually to become my wife. The area was between the towns of Brighton and Ann Arbor, Michigan. On a back road, I stopped at a stop sign where the road met a two-lane, paved road called Pontiac Trail. My destination

was ten miles south, to the small town of South Lyon, where I was living. There was no traffic. I clearly remember pulling out onto Pontiac Trail . . . and then my car was bumping over the railroad tracks at the edge of South Lyon in what seemed, literally, the blink of an eye. At that time, Pontiac Trail was a road with many hills and curves. There was no way I could have driven that distance in that terrain while asleep at the wheel. Unfortunately, I did not check the time before or after.

2. *Beyond the Light.* In the 1980s, while living in Malibu, California, I was on my way home again at night, just coming up to the crest of Point Dume on Pacific Coast Highway. On the other side of the crest, the highway went downhill, then past Zuma Beach and on up the coast of California. At the end of Zuma Beach, which was only a couple of miles long, there was a traffic light at the corner of Trancas Canyon Road. At that light I intended to turn right into the community where I lived. However, I remember coming up to the crest, and then I didn't know where I was. My speed hadn't changed, but the highway was dark and I didn't recognize it at all. Then I passed a sign giving the distance to the city of Ventura, and I realized that I was five miles (eight km) past the Trancas Canyon traffic light. (This was the same highway where, at a later date, my eldest son fell asleep at the wheel and crashed my car; it was well known for those kinds of

accidents.) That I fell asleep and drove seven miles, including a well-lit intersection, on a curving highway with other traffic is not a viable assumption.

Unexplainable events used to be reported much more frequently than they are now. A famous researcher of such events in the early twentieth century, Charles Fort, collected some forty thousand items of strange and wondrous data from scientific journals, periodicals, and newspapers. In the 1970s it was not unusual for Los Angeles newspapers to report the unusual. I still remember stories of rocks popping up out of the ground in Oklahoma and rain in the yard of a suburban Los Angeles home under clear skies. Slowly, over the years, with hardly anyone noticing, such stories have all but disappeared. Even UFO stories are very rare, although a bit of research will show that UFO-related events are still happening. There was a brief flurry of interest regarding "flying rods," but since they were explained in a satisfactory first-level way, you don't hear about them anymore. Life goes on, though, and whether these events are in the news or not, lots of things still happen that demonstrate the inherent strangeness of reality. I'll describe three of my own experiences. The first two may be rare, but the last is shared by many others.

The Dodging Dodge
In 1960, after a stint in the United States Marine Corps, I was back in college in Michigan, driving a 1949 Dodge

convertible with four bald tires. One rainy, misty morning, I was driving in the center lane of a four-lane highway between the towns of Ypsilanti and Ann Arbor. Traffic was heavy in all four lanes. Ahead of me I suddenly saw a small white car at a full stop with its left-hand turn signal blinking. I slammed on my brakes, but it was like being on ice, and I kept going without slowing down at all. A quick glance in my rearview mirror showed cars coming up behind me and on my right, and the oncoming lanes on my left were full. At the last moment before crashing into the white car in front of me, I twisted my steering wheel to the right. I don't know why I did it, but there wasn't anything else to do. By all the laws of first-level physics, the driver's side of my car ought to have smashed into the rear of the white car, the car behind me ought to have smashed into my passenger side, and the car that had been coming up on my right ought to have taken off the whole front end of my car. Instead, the moment I twisted the steering wheel, my car windows became blank white, and it felt like my car was spinning very slowly in a circle. I remember thinking, "So this is the end, is it?" Then, very suddenly, my car stopped, the windows cleared, and I was in my car, facing the original direction, off the right side of the road. On my left, four lanes of traffic were moving smoothly, as if nothing out of the ordinary had ever happened, not even a near accident. There was no sign of the small white car. I trembled for a few moments and then drove off, because there wasn't anything else to do.

The Soft and Skinny Land Rover

In the late 1960s, I was working in West Africa, and some of my work took me on safari in the Sahel and Sahara lands between Senegal and Mauritania. On one trip with three assistants, we had just crossed the border into Senegal and were heading for Dakar. It was around 8:00 p.m. and very dark. I was in the front passenger seat of my Land Rover; one of my assistants, Salif, was driving; and the other two were in the backseat. There were no seatbelts. Salif was driving at about fifty miles per hour (eighty kmph) on a dirt road when we found ourselves behind a large truck, and Salif swerved to the left to pass it on the shoulder. Suddenly (why is it always suddenly?), our headlights showed a concrete bridge railing directly ahead of us. The one-and-a-half-lane road had narrowed into a one-lane bridge, something very common on country roads. Our headlights showed a steep drop-off to the left of the bridge and the truck just beginning to get on it. At the last possible moment, when the body of the truck was on our right, Salif whipped the steering wheel to the right (is there something magical about that direction?). By objective worldview rules, we ought to have smashed into the truck and the end of the bridge railing at the same time, causing no end of damage and very probably several deaths.

What happened was different. I have no idea how we crossed the bridge, but I remember hearing a loud bang somewhere on the upper right outside of the Rover, and then the vehicle was on the other side of the bridge, off the left side of the bridge and roaring between trees until we hit one dead-on and stopped. In spite of our speed, all I felt from the impact was a small jolt. Salif sat there, unhurt, looking dazed. Looking behind me, I saw that my other two assistants and the right rear door were missing. I got out and saw the door some ways back on the ground, and then I found my two assistants sitting on the ground together some distance behind the Rover, also unhurt and looking dazed. They did not look like they had been thrown out. I went back to where the truck was stopped only partly off the bridge. The driver was standing outside it, and he was unhurt and dazed as well. I looked carefully at the part of the truck that was still on the bridge, and there was only about eighteen inches (forty-five cm) of clearance on either side. Toward the rear of the left side of the truck there was a dent at the height of a similar dent on the upper right rear of the Land Rover. The unexplainable indication was that the Land Rover had crossed the bridge at the same time as the truck. Going back to the front of the Land Rover, I found that the thick steel bumper had wrapped itself around the tree only where it had contacted the trunk, making the same shape that soft clay would make if pressed with a wooden dowel. The rest of the bumper looked normal. Was reality distorted or was matter distorted, and how and why? I don't have any answers. I could make some up, and maybe so could you, but they would only be made-up answers.

When the World Changes

This is a potentially controversial subsection, more so than any of the others, because it is so contrary to all first-level, and most second-level, logic. It's basically a third-level idea that assumes multiple intersecting dimensions of reality.

Parallel lives have been the subject of numerous science fiction and fantasy stories. For most people, the term "parallel life" implies two kinds of experience that exist side by side but do not interact. A good example occurs in the movie *Stardust* in which a stone wall separates two different "worlds" on the same planet, one very first level and one very magical. There is a break in the wall where some individuals can go back and forth, but the worlds are essentially separate. Another version of parallel lives was in the description I gave above regarding the relationship between my writer self and my artist self. I'm not talking about either of these things now.

There is no commonly accepted term for what I'm trying to describe, so I will make one up. I will call it Concurrent Fields of Reality (CFOR). The general idea is that there coexist multiple alternate versions of Life Prime, not stacked vertically, but laid out next to each other like a lot of slightly overlapping sheets of paper arranged on a very large table. The nature of Life Prime is such that each of us residing in it may slip and slide into one of these other versions without realizing it, unless we pay attention and are willing to acknowledge the possibility. Rather than try to explain it further, I think some questions will better clarify this:

- Have you ever heard people you know, and/or the media in general, suddenly using a word you've never heard before as if it were a common term that everyone ought to know?
- Have you ever walked down a familiar street and seen a new construction or a missing building that you don't remember at all?
- Have you ever had a conversation with friends or relatives that included strong disagreement about something you clearly remember?
- Have you ever awakened one morning to find that something about your body had changed dramatically?
- Have you ever discovered that things you knew you had did not exist, and/or that you now have things you're sure you never had before?

These are some of the things that may indicate that you have slid into an alternate version of Life Prime. Naturally, you wouldn't want to share this kind of experiential interpretation with everyone, because a very first-level analysis of your interpretation would be that you are having a psychotic episode. The same thing happened in nineteenth-century France when some people claimed to have found meteorites. The first-level scientists of the day scoffed at this with the following logic: "You cannot have found rocks that fall from the sky for the simple reason that rocks do not fall from the sky." According to the same logic, you cannot have slid into an alternate reality for the simple reason that you are not in an alternate reality.

Third-level logic, however, assumes that reality is a dream and that dreams can overlap. Once we accept the possibility, the next proper question is, "Can we make it happen consciously?" I believe we can, and I'm trying to find out how.

Part 5

Changing Reality in the Holistic World

I Thought of Wind

I thought of wind
And then it blew so
Swiftly through the trees.

I thought of waves
And on they came
In sparkling, moving seas.

Of birds I thought
And heard them sing
With voices wild and pure.

Of love I thought
And love was there
All strong and deep and sure.

Now I don't know
If life just is
And thoughts just guide my sight,

Or whether thoughts
Somehow attract
Experience's light.

Perhaps it's just
Some vasty dream
With inner sight I see,

Or maybe, though
It's real all right;
I'm only seeing me.

—Serge Kahili King, 2002

Chapter 12

Unity in Diversity

My Hawaiian uncle loved to tell stories as a way of explaining the concepts he was teaching me. Most of the time they were based on Hawaiian legends, and sometimes he just made them up. Occasionally, he would borrow stories from other cultures and give them a Hawaiian flavor. I think the following story is one of those.

MAUI'S QUESTION

Once upon a time, long before Captain Cook, *Maui Kupua*, Maui the Shaman, finally died after a long and adventurous life and went to *Kanehunamoku*, the hidden land of Kane, the Great Spirit. There he immediately went to sleep and rested for quite a while. When he woke up, the invisible presence of Kane was right beside him. Maui jumped up and they exchanged greetings. Then Maui felt an urge to talk to Kane about his life; and so he did, going on and on about the things he'd learned, the pranks he'd played, the beings he'd helped and the beings he'd hurt, his loves and his hates, and the good times and the bad. He talked and talked and talked until he ran out of things to say. At that moment, he shook his head as if with a sudden awareness and looked around. "Kane," he said, "where is everyone? My grandmother, my mother, my wife? My father, brothers, friends, and enemies? All my ancestors who must have come before me?"

"What do you mean?" asked Kane.

"Well," said Maui, "where are they? I don't see them anywhere. Are they in another part of the island?"

Maui felt, rather than heard, the deep, gentle laughter of Kane before the Great Spirit replied, "Oh, Maui, there never was anyone else."

A DIFFICULT LESSON

I had more trouble with this worldview than with any of the others. First Level was easy, because it came with our educational system and was reinforced all the time by our social system. Second Level was easy, too, because I had so many experiences that fit only that worldview, and because I met so many people who had similar experiences. The third-level worldview was fairly easy once I realized that dream experiences and Life Prime experiences felt the same and were remembered the same. As for Fourth Level, I had studied religions, philosophies, and avant-garde scientific theories that proposed a holistic universe, but I didn't get it on a feeling level until my uncle explained it in a different way and gave me some techniques to make it practical.

IT'S ALL ABOUT RELATIONSHIPS

One thing my uncle told me was that all the worldviews are just that: different viewpoints of how the world works. None of them represents a truer version of reality than the others, and they do not represent a hierarchy of importance. The true shaman learns to use all four according to need or desire, and even more than one at the same time if that proves useful. As he put it, "We learn to swim through different worlds." He also said, in my words, that the Holistic World is a nice place to visit, but you wouldn't want to live there because you wouldn't have any friends to party with.

In more practical terms, he told me that everyone uses all four worldviews every day without realizing it. For instance, you might have a first-level relationship with your employer or employee or a clerk in a store or a different tribe or political party in which you and they are clearly separate from each other. At the same time, you might have a second-level relationship with your spouse or your parents or your close friends, in which you are very sensitive to their thoughts, feelings, and energy levels. Still at the same time, you could have a third-level relationship to people in your life who symbolize your hopes and dreams or fears and frustrations. And, simultaneously, you might have a fourth-level relationship with your children or a loved one or an idol with whom you identify so closely that when something good or bad happens to him or her, you feel like it is happening to you.

So, the holistic worldview is not an all-or-nothing state. In shamanic thinking, it applies only to whatever you unconsciously or consciously identify with. For the rest of this chapter I will be giving you different techniques for using this worldview to change reality in many ways.

PERSONAL PROGRAMMING

The best thing about being able to shift your worldview is that it opens up a wider range of options for making changes. If you have trouble making friends, you can use a first-level approach of learning social skills, a second-level approach of helping others to be more relaxed and open around you, a third-level approach of finding and changing symbols of the problem, or a fourth-level approach of changing your perception of yourself. The fundamental assumption of fourth level is that, instead of trying to change the world, just change yourself and the world will change around you, or, rather, it will change in response to the changes you've made in yourself.

This isn't such a strange idea. We encounter it frequently in Western teaching, such as:

- To get a smile, give a smile.
- To make a friend, be a friend.
- Laugh and the world laughs with you (although the second part of this phrase is "cry and you cry alone"; you'll discover that crying makes most people around you unhappy).
- To be successful, do what successful people do.
- Fake it till you make it.

Nevertheless, it's amazing how few people use even these simple ideas. You, since you have read this far, probably want to go further than that, so here are some methods of personal programming that work.

Self-Awareness

How much attention do you pay to yourself? I don't mean the kind of so-called "self-obsession" that actually consists of thinking constantly about what other people think about you. I mean simply being passively aware of your body and your mind at different times and under different conditions. You might react at first with a statement like, "Of course, I'm aware of when my body feels good and when it hurts, and when my mind is thinking positive or negative thoughts," but I don't mean that, either. Simple awareness, without trying to change anything or without trying to interpret anything, can have a profound effect on your life. The superficial effect that you will probably notice first is stress relief. At the fourth level, however, we know that the tension in your body is directly related to the way you think and to the problems—and good things—in your life. The fourth-level solution I'm presenting here has nothing to do with getting a massage or positive thinking or dreaming good dreams. All it requires is awareness, because that is the first step to connecting, and connecting is the first step to identifying, and identifying with something inherently feels good, and the better you feel the better your world becomes.

Please stay with me now, don't lose me. At this point it is easy to slip into another worldview where how you feel doesn't change anything. If you can stay with the fourth level worldview, it does.

Here is a demonstration I do sometimes in class to illustrate this point. Having prepared myself with a long stick, I place an empty plastic water bottle where every-one can see it clearly. Then I ask them to look at it for one minute, paying attention to its color, shape, size, and label. At the one-minute mark, I knock the bottle over with the stick. Although one minute is not very long, invariably the majority of the class will have a startle reaction and report that it felt like I had poked them with the stick. That's how fast identification can happen when there is no distraction. (Those in the class who do not react are probably worrying about doing the exercise correctly.)

It's time for a technique I call Skin and Bones. You could use something else to be aware of, but I get very good results with this:

1. Take five or ten minutes out of your busy life to find a location with as few distractions as possible, especially from other people. The more time you have the better. You can do this sitting, standing, walking, or lying down, with your eyes open or closed.

2. For approximately half the time you have available, be aware of your bones. You can shift your awareness randomly—a shoulder bone here, a thigh bone there—or you can be more progressive, starting with your skull and moving downward. There isn't anything to do except be aware that the bones are there.

3. For approximately the other half of the time, be aware of your skin, either randomly or progressively. Do your best to move away from any comments, criticisms, or interpretations that your mind may make, and move back as well as you can to simple awareness that your skin exists.

4. During the process, pay attention to how your body and your mind react, and how your feelings change, as you continue.

5. After the process, pay attention to any changes that occur in your life, especially with regard to problem areas. Changes may be subtle or dramatic, immediate or delayed.

If you switch worldviews, of course, you may not make any correlations between this exercise and life changes, or you may even deny that any exist. Also, I cannot promise that doing this exercise will be pleasant at the beginning if you have a lot of tension or a lot of problems, but I do tell you that the more you do it the better it feels—even bliss is possible—and whether you make the correlations or not, both bad things and good things will get better.

Self-Relaxation

You are right, this only means to relax yourself, but I'm going to give you a special way of doing it. The effects will be similar to the last exercise. If you want a name for what we are about to do, we could call it Progressive Stretching. I'll talk only about the neck here, because a great amount of unrealized tension accumulates in this area, which inhibits a lot of mind and body functions.

1. It is easiest to do this sitting down with your hands in your lap. Start by moving your head very slowly to the right as far as you can without strain.
2. At the first sign of strain, move your head very slowly back to the left, a bit beyond the point where you started, and then again very slowly to the right, a bit beyond the point where you stopped before, until you feel a strain.

3. Repeat the above movements until you can move your head farther and farther to the right, as far as possible without strain or pain, then do the same on the left side.

4. When you are ready, continue the process forward, backward, and diagonally. It is common for spontaneous deep breathing to occur during the process, but it if doesn't, consciously take a deep breath before changing direction.

5. If you want, continue the process with your shoulders and your leg-hip joints.

Self-Focus

For every problem we have, whether it is a matter of health, personal relationships, money, or anything else, you will always find one or more areas of tension in your body that are related to it. What I am about to present is not a quick and easy technique, but it is designed to help resolve the issue. It is based on a type of passive meditation called *nalu*. Before you begin, think of a problem and put something in front of you to help you keep your mind on the problem. It could be a photograph, a drawing, a related piece of paper, or an object, such as the highest denomination bill you have available if the subject is money. Whatever you choose, for the purpose of this exercise, accept it as the problem itself, not just a symbol. And it's a good idea to decide on a word or a short phrase that you can repeat during the exercise to help you keep your focus. The more serious the problem, the more difficult it is to keep your mind on it without getting distracted. And be sure to pick a neutral word or phrase that simply describes the problem without criticism or emotion.

1. With the problem in front of you, just look at it and pay attention to what your mind does and how your body reacts. You don't have to do anything about the mental and physical reactions, because they will change by themselves the longer you look at the problem.
2. While you are looking at the problem, do this special kind of breathing: inhale with attention on the problem; exhale with attention on the part of your body that reacts the most strongly; then inhale with attention on that part of the body and exhale with attention on the problem. Repeat this cycle during the whole process.
3. Do the exercise for as long as you can, and repeat the exercise as often as you can, until you begin to think and feel differently about the problem without making any effort to do so. At this point, changes and opportunities in relation to the problem will begin to appear in your life.

Self-Presence

The technique given in this section will help to increase your confidence, your energy, and the influence of your thoughts, feelings, and actions on the world around you. And all this comes about from increasing your own sensory presence. This one can be practiced any time, anywhere, under any conditions.

1. In your current environment, look at details of color, shape, position, movement, and spatial relationships between objects and people.
2. In your current environment, listen to all the various sounds and subdivisions of sounds that you can hear. For instance, you may hear the wind, but if you listen closely you will find that the wind is composed of many sounds.
3. In your current environment, touch things that are nearby and feel the differences in texture, temperature, and weight.
4. In your current environment, when you move, move deliberately, with full awareness of your body.
5. Do all these things simultaneously if you can, or at least in close sequence. Pay attention to if and how the world responds to your presence.

Self-Appreciation

The way you think about yourself is the way the world will think about you. The worth you give yourself is the worth the world will grant you. The world will not appreciate you at a higher degree than that at which you appreciate yourself. And when you have mixed feelings about yourself, the world will have mixed feelings about you. What your conscious mind, your focus mind, would *like* the world to think about you doesn't have nearly as much effect as what your focus mind really expects and what your body mind really believes. If you want more appreciation from the world in any form, you must start giving it to yourself. The technique for this section is simplicity itself. Most people find it very difficult to do and maintain, though.

1. Start every morning with a personal review of all your good qualities, all the good things you've done, and all the good things you plan to do (or at least as many as you can think of or have the time for). The world, which is always listening, doesn't want to hear about what you think are your faults, your failures, and your mistakes.

2. End every day with a review of all the good qualities you expressed and all the good things you did that day. If you are interested in financial appreciation, write yourself a symbolic check to yourself for what you think your day was worth, and if it was an especially good day, give yourself a bonus. The world, which is always listening and watching, doesn't care about what you think you could have done better or should have done right. It cares only about what you think about what you did do.

Self-Empowerment

The most effective way to empower yourself is to increase your personal sovereignty. Personal sovereignty is an issue that affects each of us as individuals and as a society, whether we realize it or not. Understanding it can help us interpret what is going on within us and around us. Increasing it can radically transform our existence.

The word *sovereign* means to be in supreme authority over someone or something and to be extremely effective and powerful. Therefore, it is usually applied to gods, royalty, and governments. We speak of kings and queens as sovereigns (even when they are figureheads) and of the sovereign rights of nations and states.

Personal sovereignty, then, would imply the intrinsic authority and power of an individual to determine his or her own direction and destiny. If that sounds suspiciously like free will, it's because personal sovereignty and free will are the same thing.

Just as being a sovereign nation means having the right and power to make decisions and take actions in the national interest without being forced to by another nation, so being a sovereign person means being able to choose one's actions and reactions without being forced to by another person. To the degree that there is free will in all such choices, national or personal, there is sovereignty.

Although having sovereignty also means to be powerful and effective, it doesn't necessarily follow that once you have it you can do anything you want. Whether you are a nation or a person, you also have to consider the sovereignty of others. Of course, you could try to diminish or destroy the sovereignty of others to get what you want, the way nations and people sometimes do, but human experience shows that you can usually accomplish more by cooperating than by conquering.

Ultimately, however, we each have only as much sovereignty as we can demonstrate. Having sovereign rights and being sovereign are not the same thing.

The way to increase your personal sovereignty is to increase your use of free will, and here is how to do that:

1. Decide for yourself what actions to take and reactions to have in any situation.
2. Decide for yourself how to interpret your actions and reactions whether they are freely chosen or not.

For instance, if you work for someone and are ordered to do an unpleasant task, it can feel like you have lost some of your free will. But in addition to remembering that you can always quit, you can also decide for yourself that you are not working for the boss; you are providing a compensated service, and you can decide to do the task because you choose to, not because you are ordered to. The point is that you can always choose your actions and reactions and interpretations.

Beware, though. Personal sovereignty has a high price. It's called personal responsibility. As you increase your use of free will, you also increase your responsibility for your own actions and reactions. Increase it enough and you won't be able to blame your parents, your enemies, your friends, your lovers or spouse, society, fate, Satan, or God for anything having to do with your experience. And you will feel more powerful and be more powerful in your effects on the world.

If a lot of people were to greatly increase their personal responsibility, our society would undergo tremendous change. Codependent and manipulative relationships would all but disappear; untold numbers of trial lawyers would have to find new professions; politicians would be held accountable for their decisions; insurance companies would have to change many of their policies; people of different faiths would be more tolerant of each other; humanity would act more from love than fear . . . Now what kind of world would that be? A very good one, I think.

Self-Harmony

If we understand these two words individually, it will be easier to understand them when used as a single phrase. *Harmony* is easy to understand, because it comes from the Latin, *harmonius*, which means "joined, in agreement." *Self* is a word that normally refers to an individual as distinct from a group. In Huna, though, we often use the term "three selves" in reference to the grouping of body, mind, and spirit in one individual. Since we don't mean that body, mind, and spirit are three separate individuals, a better term would be "three aspects of one self." Nevertheless, in some people these three aspects seem to be at war with one another, and war within the individual is directly related to war around the individual. Also, war is always based on fear. And fear is always based on disharmony, or, more accurately, the feeling of being disconnected from a source of love and/or power. And that feeling all too often leads to anger, which creates more disconnection. The solution, therefore, is to reconnect. There are two Hawaiian proverbs that express these concepts more poetically:

'Akahi a komo ke anu ia'u, ua naha ka hale e malu ai
Cold now penetrates me, for the house that protects is broken

By tradition, this was said by an ancient chief to express the fear that he felt when his two war leaders were killed in a battle.

Pili kau, pili ho'oilo
Together in the dry season, together in the wet season

This is a proverb that describes a loving relationship.

I am leading up to the point that in order to have harmony within you and around you, you must make peace with yourself. And the way to make peace with yourself is to make friends with yourself.

In case you are wondering, the way to make friends with anyone is to appreciate them and empower them, *from a position of self-appreciation and self-empowerment*. So the next step is to learn how to do that. I'm going to give you one technique here, and you can learn a lot more about the subject in my book *Healing Relationships*.

1. Pretend that you are the captain of a sports team or the leader of a band, and the members of your group are called Spirit, Mind, and Body. Your purpose is to become friends so that you can work together in complete harmony.

2. First, tell the members what they are supposed to do. You can say something like, "Spirit, we need inspiration and energy; Mind, get whatever information you need and find solutions to our problems; Body, remember what you know how to do, relax, and feel good."

3. Second, appreciate whatever they do that increases your effectiveness, and forgive whatever they do that doesn't. You can say something like, "Spirit, that was a good idea, thank you; Mind, I like the way you used your imagination on that one; Body, thank you for cooperating." Rewarding your selves with a special treat appropriate to each one is also a good thing to do.

4. Remind them and yourself as captain/leader that friends do not criticize each other or work against each other.

As you continue this exercise and your inner harmony increases, you'll need to do it less and less, and the day will come when you and your group are really one.

Chapter 13

A Time to Grok

R obert A. Heinlein, a writer known mostly for his science fiction stories, coined the word *grok* in his 1961 novel, *Stranger in a Strange Land*. The protagonist, Valentine Michael Smith, was raised by Martians, and on page 14 Heinlein first mentions the word in a casual way as he writes about Smith's "grokking that he was not as his nestling brothers," referring to the moment on Mars when he used a special kind of talent to realize that he was not a Martian.

In a modern dictionary, *grok* is defined as meaning "to understand something intuitively or by empathy" and "to empathize or communicate sympathetically; to establish a rapport." Well, that may be how a lot of people are using it today, but that's only part of the meaning Heinlein gave it in the novel. One clue to the full meaning is given on page 105, where Smith comments on a woman's ability to swim by saying, "The water groks Dorcas. It cherishes (her)." Smith chooses his words very carefully, and *cherish* means "to protect and care for someone lovingly." In the rest of the chapter, Heinlein, through dialogue, makes it clear that the concept of grokking includes to know something from the inside—much more than just in the sense of empathy—and, while in that state of knowing, to be able to influence what you are grokking. In addition, "grokking in fullness" means to become one with something.

The skill of grokking is well known to shamans, but it isn't easy to convey through modern languages. It isn't unknown; it just isn't easy to explain. A close approximation of grokking can be found in the technique of Method Acting, based on the teachings of Lee Strasberg and Konstantin Stanislavski. An anonymous article, quoted widely on the Web, says that "Method Acting combines a careful consideration of the psychological motives of the character, and some sort of personal identification with and possibly the reproduction of the character's emotional state in a realistic way."

Modern discussions on shamanism approach the subject obliquely or partially, with their emphasis on form rather than function. In these discussions, the subject is called "shapeshifting" or "shapechanging," and there is generally a recognition of three types: a change in how one appears to others; a visible spirit form that may or may not be human (like I described in chapter 9 in the soul-retrieval section); and an actual physical transformation (like a werewolf). When I lived in West Africa, the people of Dahomey/Benin were firmly convinced that the president of the country could take the form of an antelope in order to spy on them.

Grokking, however, as described by Heinlein and practiced by shamans, does not require a change in appearance or form. What it does require is the ability to know, merge with, and influence a pattern.

PATTERNS

We are all familiar with patterns of some kind.

- People who sew are familiar with clothing patterns.
- Meteorologists are familiar with weather patterns.
- Psychologists are familiar with behavioral patterns.
- Geologists are familiar with rock patterns.
- Civil engineers are familiar with stress patterns.
- City managers are familiar with traffic patterns.
- Mathematicians are familiar with fractal patterns.

And on and on.

The more familiar we are with patterns, the more we "incorporate" them (bring them into our body); and that incorporation allows us, not only to use the pattern at will, but also to improvise upon it in creative ways and even to use our knowledge of the pattern to influence something else that uses the pattern.

Musicians are very familiar with this idea. Mozart was a master of the musical patterns of his day, and he could instantly recognize the pattern of any piece of music he heard, reproduce it, and improvise on it to create something new. When I first began to play the ukulele, I learned a number of simple chord patterns that could be used to play hundreds of songs, and I even wrote songs for those patterns. Many artists use patterns, as do many writers and speakers and computer game designers. Our life is full of patterns that people learn and use to change reality.

Natural Patterns

Some of the most interesting patterns, in my opinion, are found in nature. We recognize the difference between ferns and trees because of trunk and branch and leaf patterns, and we use the same categories of patterns to distinguish among trees. At the same time, many trees have leaf patterns that are similar to ferns. And some trees, like koa, have one leaf pattern resembling a fern when they are young and undergo a transformation to another leaf pattern that resembles a eucalyptus when they mature. Yet, the woody part of a koa tree more closely resembles that of a mahogany.

Ocean waves form patterns that are strongly influenced by wind patterns and land patterns, and at the same time, if you look closely, you'll see that waves have waves that are influenced by waves.

One of the most incredible patterns in nature has been mathematically defined as a relationship of numbers called "The Golden Mean." I'm not going to turn this into a mathematical lesson, and nature isn't very precise anyway, so in the simplest possible approximate terms, many things in nature are constructed, or construct themselves, by using a pattern related to the number 1.618, called *phi.* For example, I am 70 inches (178 cm) tall, and my navel is 42 inches (107 cm) above the ground. If we divide 70 by 1.618, we get 43 inches (109 cm). If you are wondering what that has to do with anything, let's go further. The length from the tip of my middle finger on my left hand to my shoulder point is 28 inches (71 cm), and if we divide that by 1.618 the result is 17 inches (43 cm). The length from my middle finger to my elbow is 18 inches. The distance from my navel to the top of my head is 28 inches (71 cm), and the result of dividing that by 1.618 is 17 inches (43 cm), the same distance as from my navel to the top of my breastbone. This close relationship between body parts and the number 1.618 can be found in all human bodies, as well as in seashells, crystals, fruit, leaves, and lots and lots of other things. Humans use it on purpose in art and architecture. In nature it isn't perfect, but it's close.

The point is that patterns are everywhere, and patterns can be used.

When I play certain songs on the ukulele, or sing them; when I dance certain dances; when I drive to certain locations; when I sail certain kinds of boats; when I use certain kinds of computers, I don't have to think about what I'm doing, because the pattern is part of me. In a sense, we have merged. In order to express the pattern, though, I have to make a conscious decision to merge with it, by picking up the ukulele, getting into the boat, etc. Then I can let the pattern guide me. Or I can guide the pattern into potentials that modify or expand the pattern without changing it.

Let me use the ukulele as an example. I can play a song called "Ain't She Sweet" without paying any attention to what my hands are doing. Or, I can purposely linger on certain chords, add other chords, change the rhythm or the key—all without changing the song. I can do so because the song has a range of possible modifications that can be made within its overall pattern. If I go out of that range, however, by playing chords to which the pattern will not adapt, I will either be playing a different song or just be making noise.

This is exactly what is involved in using patterns to change reality. The holistic worldview says that because everything is one, anything can become one with anything else. The way we do that is by merging patterns on a deeper level. In other words, we merge with the inner pattern of something—the pattern that gives rise to its existence, not merely the pattern that it expresses in its behavior.

Inner Patterns

There is a very ancient idea that the whole universe is made out of the same basic stuff. I don't mean atomic or subatomic particles, and I don't mean the early nineteenth-century concept of the "light-bearing ether," which was itself considered to be a physical substance. The idea that I'm trying to express is something like "pre-matter," an infinite, nonmaterial matrix, the "mother of all patterns." A further idea is that all of creation arises out of this matrix—let's call it a field—by a means about which we don't have to trouble ourselves. We could, of course, but then I'd just be writing a book about theories. Let's jump past all that the theories and just assume the existence of such a field. A Hawaiian name for it would be *aka*, probably related to the Sanskrit, *akasia*. The meanings given for *aka* in the Hawaiian dictionary are relevant: "shadow," "reflection," "image," "likeness," "essence," "clarity," "an embryo at the point of conception," "a newly hatched fish in the stage where its body is still transparent." The relationship to patterns is inherent in the phrase, *aka lehulehu*, "shadow of the multitude," a figurative way of saying "a well-worn path." Aka, then, is *the* pattern, out of which all other patterns emerge.

Without getting complicated, we can say that patterns emerge by means of movement or energy. Since we are working with the holistic worldview, we don't have to worry about First Cause, a very objective worldview concept. For all we know and for all that matters, energy and aka have always existed, and patterns are formed by energy interfering with energy. Using concepts with which you are already familiar, energy is like the focus mind, and aka is like the body mind. Energy "imagines" (or creates) new patterns, and aka remembers them. We can say, therefore, that the whole universe consists of patterns and energy, patterns of energy, and energized patterns. It is because of this underlying field and flow of which we are a part that we can merge and modify.

FINALLY, THE PRACTICAL STUFF

Before we can merge with the world around us, we have to know how to merge. It's a lot easier than you might think, because you do it so often already without thinking about it. Here, I will organize this natural process into steps so you can engage in it more consciously.

1. Get to know what you want to merge with. The more intellectual and experiential knowledge you have about something, the easier it is to know the pattern in an intuitive way. There's a proverb that says, "Familiarity breeds contempt." That's a lie. It is loss of respect that breeds contempt. Familiarity actually breeds connection.

2. Make friends with what you want to merge with. If you don't like something, or you are afraid of it, you won't be able to connect very well with the pattern. Knowledge can help to change that. The easiest way to make friends with anything is to assume that

it's alive and talk to it with compliments, praise, and admiration.

3. Practice imagining and feeling that you actually are the thing you want to merge with. You may find it easier to start by focusing on a symbol of the thing at your navel. In my classes I sometimes speak about keeping the "one percent shaman" when you merge, meaning never to merge more than ninety-nine percent, because if you merge 100 percent, you'll forget about trying to have any influence. In actual practice, however, you will rarely ever merge more than 25 percent, but even this much will give you a considerable degree of influence.

4. When you are merged to whatever degree, let your mind and your feelings explore existing potentials for modifying the pattern. For instance, if you think of a modification you desire, pay attention to ideas and feelings of resistance or flow. You cannot make anything do what it does not have the desire or potential to do.

One important thing to understand in grokking for change is that, in addition to the fact that you can work only with existing potentials, you are never working alone. There will always be someone or something else cooperating, helping, or resisting the change, so you can never take full credit for success or blame for failure. All you can do— and it's a good thing to do—is the best you can.

All of the examples below have to do with grokking in order to help and to heal others. Please keep in mind that you can also grok anyone or anything to increase your own knowledge, skills, and well-being.

WORKING THE PATTERNS

We are going to use a Hawaiian shamanic practice of dividing the world into seven "elements." This way we can learn how to grok for many types of problems. Each element will have its own section with guidelines, examples, and comments. The order of presentation is not hierarchical.

Water Grokking

Qualities you can grok include flow, absorption, adaptability, and persistent action. Water-related problems to work with include excessive rain, floods, tides, drought, clouds, and water supply.

Examples

1. I helped bring rain to a Texas valley during a drought one time. Significantly, the whole state was suffering from a drought, but after a few days we were able to bring a good rainfall to that one valley.
2. Friends and I grokked a tsunami headed for Kauai from Japan with official warnings that it was going

to be a bad one. Needless to say, all the people who gathered to watch it were very disappointed when nothing happened. We work with every tsunami headed toward Hawaii that we hear of, and since we began doing this, there has not been a single one that has done any damage (except for one when our focus was on a different part of the island).

3. The month of November is well into the rainy season on Kauai. For eighteen years, we held an annual outdoor festival on the American Thanksgiving Day on the rainy side of the island, and partly due to our grokking efforts we were rained out only once.

4. Clouds are fun to work with because they are so responsive. Many times I have grokked and guided clouds away from picnics or brought them in when we needed shade.

5. With floods, I find it useful to become the moving water and try to find the least-damaging channels to flow into.

6. I have done a small amount of successful water dowsing by "feeling" where the water was. There is a dowsing technique of diverting an underground stream by pounding a metal post into the ground at the point where the stream is entering and flooding a building. I did this once a little differently by placing a thoughtform of a post and then grokking the water to divert myself away from the thoughtform, and the flooding stopped.

Stone Grokking

Qualities you can grok include strength, security, patience, and firmness. Stone-related problems to work with include earthquakes, landslides, volcanoes, erosion, and soil.

Examples

1. We do a lot of work with earthquakes in the Pacific Basin, most often with diminishing the effect of after-shocks as much as we can, since initial earthquakes don't give much warning. Recently we had some sharp quakes on the Big Island close to Kilauea Volcano, and our work was so effective that the United States Geological Service reported a very unusual day when only one small quake was recorded in a twenty-four-hour period, while the norm is to have many small quakes every day of the year. The way we usually work is to grok the rocks in the earthquake zone, feel where the tension is, and relax.

2. With landslides and erosion we seek to stabilize an area, and with soil we may try to alter the chemical composition for the purpose at hand.

3. In 1990, lava from craters on the side of Kilauea Volcano on the Big Island was headed for the village of Kalapana on the ocean. A friend whose home was in danger asked me to do what I could to keep the lava away from her house. In grokking, I decided, as the lava, not to touch her house. Later she told

me that the lava flowed right by her house without touching it, but because her house was surrounded by the lava and all utilities were cut off, she had to abandon it.

Fire Grokking

Qualities you can grok include energy, intensity, changeability, awareness, and action. Fire-related problems to work with include fires, heat, cold, darkness, and light.

Examples

1. Forest fires are the most common thing we work with in this category. When working with fire directly, I grok the fire, feel the happy rush of energy, then decide to calm down, turn into embers and finally into simple heat that merges with the ambient temperature. Friends and I have been able to diminish the spread of many fires to the point where firefighters on the ground could complete the work more easily. Some people have a very hard time grokking fire because of memories or associations; it is also possible to work on fires by diminishing the wind or bringing in rain.

2. Ambient temperature change is fairly easy to do. In a number of workshops, when the temperature in a room was too hot or too cold, I have been able

to get the whole class to grok the air and change the temperature up or down, and once in New York our class influenced the temperature of the city. It helps to know that as air molecules move faster, they give off more heat, and as they move more slowly we feel that as cold. If you grok the air molecules and slow them down or speed them up, the effect is a noticeable change in temperature. This works best when a group of people are doing it.

3. When you are working with light and darkness, you must understand that they are relative to each other. In normal circumstances, even when it seems absolutely dark to a human being, some light still exists that animals and electronic-sensing equipment can see. In fact, there are even some people who are sensitive enough to see light where others cannot. In grokking light, you can think of it as a pattern of particles or as a pattern of waves; it really doesn't matter. Personally, I like to think of it as a field pattern. When I want to make changes, I also think of a pattern of intensity, which is more of a feeling pattern than a visual pattern. In some classes, I demonstrate this by grokking my personal energy field and intensifying it enough so that the audience can visually see my aura grow brighter. In a similar way, we can brighten our field or an object to make it more noticeable to people nearby, or dim it to make ourselves or an object less noticeable.

Wind Grokking

Qualities you can grok include energy, direction, adaptability, and movement. Wind-related problems to work with include hurricanes, tornadoes, storms and winds of all kinds, stillness, high and low pressure systems, and air in general.

Examples

1. My colleagues and I have had many successes with redirecting hurricanes or diminishing their strength by grokking, but remember, that works only when those potentials already exist within the hurricane itself. When you grok a hurricane, it's as if you become aware, for instance, that you are moving in one direction, and you could move to the right, but there's no way you are going to go left. As a grokker, trying to make the hurricane go left anyway would just be wasted effort. Hurricanes are so powerful that the energy scares some people, in which case they are better off working at a symbolic or subject (telepathic) level. Tornadoes are so short-lived that I have not had any opportunity to work with them, but if I lived in a tornado-prone area I would certainly practice my grokking skills.

2. Wind that is less than hurricane or tornado intensity is also easy to work with because it is so sensitive to influence. A group I was in grokked a big storm that

was headed into California from the Pacific, wanting it to back off. The next day the weather section of a news program on television displayed a map showing that the storm had actually stopped and reversed course. I remember the weatherman saying that he had never seen anything like that before. Yesterday I was working outside with some friends near Volcano Village on the Big Island of Hawaii during a period of heavy "vog" (volcanic smog) and no wind. I grokked the air, adopted a playful attitude, and decided to move. A few minutes later, a light breeze picked up and cleared our particular area of the vog, while friends living nearby said that their area remained heavily polluted. However, two hours after that, the wind brought clouds and very heavy rain to clear the air all around us, on a day when no rain was predicted by first-level sources.

Plant Grokking

Qualities you can grok include growth, expansion, nourishing, persistence, and transformation. Plant-related problems to work with include healing, growth, adaptability, and nourishment.

Examples

1. Grokking plants is a wonderful experience in and of itself, but it can also be used to find out what's

wrong if a plant is ailing and to do something about it. Sometimes what you have to do is strictly First Level: give it more water or nutrients. But sometimes it needs more loving attention from Second Level or a healing dream from Third Level. In learning about plants in general, I found out that they, like animals and humans, can get so stressed that they become more susceptible to insects, disease, and environmental conditions. Stress creates tension, so at Fourth Level, I grok the plant and relax, then open myself up to more nourishment from air, light, and soil. I do something similar when I want seeds or seedlings to grow stronger and faster.

2. Another interesting discovery I made was that plants are very sensitive to their environment and that they care about their position in relation to it. So, whenever I am planting a plant, I grok it to determine which way it wants to "face" when I put it into the ground, and it appreciates that by growing better. On occasion I have grokked a plant that is already in the ground but not doing well, and have dug it up and re-positioned it with very good results. Sometimes I will help a plant adapt to a new and different environment by grokking it and doing something that I can only describe as "adjusting its nature" so that it can adapt better.

3. In shamanic thinking, everything is alive, so there is no such thing as "dead" vegetables, cooked or not. Still, because of the way they were prepared, I may

find it useful to grok some vegetables on my plate to energize them and increase their flavor and nutrient value.

Animal Grokking

Qualities you can grok include any qualities specific to particular kinds of animals. Animal-related problems to work with include healing, energy, strength, and peacefulness.

Examples

1. When animals get sick, grokking is a very good supplemental aid to their healing. Not only can you find out more about the internal reasons or factors relating to the illness or discomfort, you can also energize their natural healing functions and help eliminate toxins faster. You can also help resolve emotional problems that are contributing to the illness. On one dramatic occasion, I grokked a dying kitten in this way and helped to bring it back to health and liveliness in one hour. I did the same for a wild bird, too sick to fly, that some friends found in a forest and brought to me. In that case it took several hours before the bird was able to fly away on its own.

2. Animals suffer a lot from emotional stress, most commonly in response to the emotional state of the people around them, to excessive changes in their

living conditions, to a lack of love, or to confusion about their role. I've mentioned how I applied the ideas of Cesar Millan by bringing myself into a state of calm confidence, but I often modify the process by grokking a wise, confident animal or the calm, confident owner of an animal to get the same relaxation of tension from the animals I want to influence. I can also grok the animal to relieve a lot of tension, but there are so many environmental factors involved that such help is too often temporary unless you are able to effect an attitude change in the animal.

Human Grokking

Qualities you can grok inlcude any qualities, talents, or skills associated with any particular human, actual or fictional. Human-related problems to work with include healing illness, stress, tension, emotions, doubt, and confusion.

Examples

1. One of the problems with grokking other humans for healing is that they are so much like us. What I mean by this is that if you want to use grokking to help someone with cancer or a broken leg, you have to be willing to experience the cancer or broken leg while in the grok and be able to give it up when you come out of it. If you are afraid of the condition someone else has,

or if you feel insecure about it, don't grok. Do something else to help. Use a different worldview. There is absolutely no danger of your developing the other person's problem by grokking, but if you were fearful enough of the condition, your body mind could take that as direction to mimic it. The other problem is that your fear would cause you to "pop out of the grok." In other words, you would be ineffective because you couldn't maintain the identification. That's okay; there are lots of other ways to help someone.

2. I have used grokking so often to help people that, rather than naming cases, I will give you a specific process for doing it adapted from the Dynamind Technique (see my book *Healing for the Millions*).

   a. Take a deep breath and relax as much as you can.

   b. Think about a person you want to help and think about the condition that person wants to change.

   c. Imagine you are that person with that condition. Take as long as you need until you can feel as much as possible that you really *are* that person, and say to yourself, "I am (name)."

   d. *As that person*, make a statement using this formula, substituting words of your choice as appropriate: "I have a problem, and that can change; I want that problem to go away and be replaced by something better."

   e. Tap your chest gently seven times; with your palm facing downward tap on top of the web of skin between your thumb and forefinger seven times on both hands; tap on the bone on the back of the base of your neck seven times.

f. Bring your hands together, inhale deeply with your attention on top of your head, and exhale deeply with your attention below your feet. Feel how your body has responded and repeat as desired.

g. When you are finished, say to yourself, "I am (your own name)" and you are finished.

And so is this book. (Actually, there's another poem and a little bit about me still to come.)

It's been a great pleasure sharing these ideas with you, partly because I love to share ideas and partly because the writing has brought back memories of things long forgotten and brought in things I never thought about before. I hope you have enjoyed it, too, but mostly I hope that you will use this book, my other books, and any other resource you can find to help to make this world a better place.

There Is a Me

There is a me not far away who's self-assured and wise;
Who always knows just what to do no matter what he tries.

He has no doubts about his worth, no fears of what's to be.
He moves ahead with confidence, this other self that's me.

This nearby self treats money as a spiritual tool.
He never lacks because for him abundance is the rule.

He loves the weak, he loves the strong, he's tolerant and kind.
He never once forgets that all effects proceed from mind.

He's able to adjust his thoughts to heal himself, and tell
The others whom he meets the way to heal themselves as well.

A skilled adept of inner space; a master smith of dreams;
He's everything I want to be and find so hard, it seems.

But he is me, and I am he. We're not so far apart.
I can make all his talents mine; I've only got to start.

The keys are Water, Air and Earth, and never-ending Fire.
I'll translate that: it's feeling, thinking, focus and desire.

—Serge Kahili King, 1979

Index

A

accountability, 291

acting, 18. *See also* Method Acting

active

    programming, 259–63

    telepathy, 69, 75–82

acupuncture/acupressure, 14

affirmations, 16

airline computer error example, 257–58

aka fields, 301–2

Aksakof, Alexander N., 151

alcohol consumption, and brain physiology, 44–45

Aloha, 22, 24, 25, 31–32

Aloha International, 119, 222

alternate-body method of magical flight, 238–39

amulets, 16

analysis, telepathic, 88

animals

    grokking, 312–13

    telepathic projection, 114–17

    thoughtform projection, 147

anthropologist example, 8–9

anxiety

    telepathic, 98

    thoughtform projection, 147

apparitions, 60, 225, 240

appreciation of self, 287–88

archeology example, 40

art

    depictions of auras, 128–29

    language of, 177

assisted levitation, 155–59

assisted object movement, 123, 166–69

assisting others through magical flight, 241–43

assumptions, 7

    holistic worldview, 17

    legacy of language, 45–46, 49

    objective worldview, 9–12

    shifting mindsets, 20

    subjective worldview, 12–13, 152

    symbolic worldview, 15–16

    telepathic projection, 111

astral projection, 219. *See also* magical flight

astrology, 14

Atlantis, 229

attention

    directed, 76. *See also* active telepathy

    focus, 75, 92

    influencing through magical flight, 241

    spontaneous, 240

attitudes, 7

auditory telepathy, 73–74
auraboards, 125, 136–38
auras, 12, 13, 125–26, 142–43, 148–49
  historical perspectives, 128–29
  increasing, 138–39, 308
  nimbus, 132–33
  as optical illusions, 138
  scientific perspectives, 129–31
  sensing, 126–28
  symbols, changing, 181
  techniques for seeing, 139–42, 148–49
  thoughtform projection, 143–48
avoidance, telepathic, 98, 99, 100
awareness, 23, 24, 25
  self, 281–84
  shifts in, 4, 39. *See also* experience
  what you see is what you get story, 26–27

B
baby, soul retrieval of, 196
Bach, Richard, 252
Bali Hai, 202
beaming, 109–13
Beckwith, Martha, 236
Beethoven's Fifth Symphony, 177
beginning and endings assumptions, 11
belief patterns, 16
bending metal, 152, 159–61
bioenergy. *See* energy
birds, communication with, 115

bleed-over/bleed-through, telepathy, 97, 101
blue color transmission, 145
bodily feedback, 180
body, as aspect of self, 291–92, 293
body mind, 62–64, 301
brain physiology, 44–45, 54
breathing exercises, 68, 85, 108, 109, 286
briefcase example, 260–61
Bristol, Claude M., 164–65
broadcasting, 106–9
Burr, Harold S., 130–31
bus, happy, 120–22

C
calm-assertive states, 117
cat coincidence, 255
causality assumptions, 11
Center of the Cyclone, The (Lilly), 223
centering, 102
Cesar's Way (Millan), 116–17
CFOR (concurrent fields of reality), 272–74
changing dreams, 175
changing reality, 35. *See also* experience
  holistic world, 275–316
  objective world, 37–54
  subjective world, 55–169
  symbolic world, 171–274, 172
changing symbols, 175
channeling, 19
Chaplin, Charlie, 143
charisma, 108, 127

choices, telepathic, 88
Christ, union with, 230
clairvoyance, 13, 222. *See also* ESP;
    subjective world; telepathy
cloud images, 145
coincidence, 82, 251–55
cold flame auras, 133, 141
color transmission, 144–47
communication, telepathic, 13,
    64–65, 89, 104–5. *See also*
    language; telepathy
    with animals, 114–17
    with nature/natural world,
    4, 12–13
    with objects, 119–23
    with weather, 117–19
computer programming
    metaphor, 256
concentration
    and emotional energy, 169
    and magical flight, 243, 247
    telekinesis, 166
concurrent fields of reality
    (CFOR), 272–74
confidence, 52
    exercises, 286
connectedness, 12–14, 18. *See also*
    grokking; unity
    and familiarity, 302
    and telepathy, 89
    three selves, 291–92
conscious awareness/
    consciousness.
    See focus mind
conversing. *See* communication;
    language

cooperative fan example, 122
cosmic consciousness, 17
counter programs, telepathy, 93
counting method of magical
    flight, 237–38
creating reality, 6–7
creative self, 199
creativity
    and brain physiology, 45
    legacy of language, 46
    and telepathy, 87
Crookes radiometer, 163–64
crossover, telepathic, 97–98
crystal balls, 84–85
crystals, 14

D
Dangerous Journeys (King), 23, 196,
    208–15, 248–49
daydreams, 60
    telepathic, 72. *See also* ESP
dead people, meeting, 227
death, 13, 14
decision-making
    mental strength, 52
    telepathic, 88
definitions
    auras, 126
    divination, 83–84
    grokking, 295
    levitation effect, 154
    reality, changing, 65
    telepathy, 65
dehydration. *See* hydration
déja vu, 60. *See also* ESP
delayed reception, telepathic, 98

dendrites, brain, 44–45, 54
Descartes, René, 17
development, self, 244–45
diagnosis of illness. *See* medical
	diagnosis
directing others, using magical
	flight, 242
distance communication.
	See communication,
	telepathic
distortion
	and magical flight, 246–47
	telepathic, 95–96
distraction, and magical flight,
	247–49
divination, 83–90
do it now, 25, 30–31
dogs
	communication with, 116–17
	thoughtform projection, 147
Donne, John, 85
dowsing, 305
	remote, 89–90
dream method of magical flight,
	231–32
dream structures, 187–88
dreamlets, 184
dreams, 15, 16, 60, 173, 278.
	See also ESP; symbolic
	worldview
	changing, 175, 179–88
	frequency patterns, 246–47
	garden symbol, 188, 189–92
	interpretation, 176–78
	lucid, 231–32
	and reality, 174–75

soul retrieval, 188,
	192–215, 199
drought, 118, 304–5
Dumas, Alexander, 47
Dynamind Technique, 43, 116, 314

E
Earth Energies (King), 69, 86, 89
earthquakes, 306
"Electro-Dynamic Theory of Life,
	The" (Burr), 130
Emerson, Ralph Waldo, 19
emotional distortion,
	telepathic, 95
emotional energy, power of,
	259–60
	bending metal, 159–60
	levitation effect, 156, 158
	and magical flight, 223
	moving objects, 162
	telekinesis, 154, 166, 167
	telepathic projection, 107, 108,
		109, 117
emotional static, 94
emotional trauma, 44
emotions
	experiencing, 13
	expression, 47
empathetic telepathy, 70–71
empathy, 19, 80, 296
empowerment, self, 289–91
energy (life force), 301. *See also*
	emotional energy
	communication with animals,
		116–17
	and ESP, 67–69

exercises, 109, 286
fields. *See* auras
focus, 109
physical, 51, 54
energy balancing, 14
energy bodies, 240
English language, 46–50
enthusiasm, telepathic
projection, 108
E-Prime, 48
erosion, soil, 306
ESP (extended sensory perception/
projection), 57–61
body mind/focus mind, 62–64
and energy, 67–69
sixth sense, 61–62
evaluation, telepathic, 88
everything is one, 17. *See also*
connectedness; unity
exaggeration, telepathic, 96, 100
exercise, physical, 51
exercises
breathing, 68, 85, 108, 109, 286
holistic worldview, 280–93
telepathy, 68, 78–80, 81, 85,
92–93
expectations, 7
experience
of emotions, 13
shamanic, 6–8
shifts in, 4
as teacher, 5
experience, influencing. *See also*
changing reality
coincidence, 251–55
matter, malleable, 263–72

parallel lives, 272–74
programming, 256–63
experiments, telepathy, 99–101
expertise, 25
extended sensory perception/
projection. *See* ESP
exterior symbols, 180–84

F
familiarity, and connection, 302
fan, cooperative, 122
fantasy stories, 26
fantasyland, 229
fear, and magical flight, 246
feedback, bodily, 180
feelings, and ESP, 58
field patterns, 301–2, 308
fields of consciousness, 224
fifth *Huna Kupua* principle, 191
filters, telepathic, 96
fire grokking, 307–8
fire, secret of story, 33–34
fireworks (auras), 135–36
First Cause, 301
first level experience. *See* objective
worldview
fishhook symbol, 25, 29–30
flashes (auras), 133–34
flight, magical. *See* magical flight
Flossie, Hurricane, 258–59
focus, 23, 24, 25
energy, 109
keep your eyes on the goal story,
29–30
self, 285–86
and telepathy, 75, 86, 92

focus mind, 54, 62–64, 102, 301
 projection, telepathic, 222
 self-appreciation, 288
 symbols, changing, 180
fog image, 145
Fort, Charles, 268
fourth level experience.
 See holistic worldview
free will, 290–91
freedom, 23, 24, 25, 28
frequency patterns, dreams, 246–47
friends, making, 280–81, 292–93
full surround auras, 134
'funny air', 239, 240
furnace repairman example, 42

G
garden symbol, 188, 189–92
ghosts, 60, 225, 240
God within you, 20
gold color transmission, 145, 147
Golden Mean, 299
green color transmission, 145, 146
grokking, 295–97. *See also*
 connectedness; unity
 and healing, 19, 313–15
 methods, 302–15
 patterns, 297–301
group chair lift, 157–58
growth, soul retrieval, 196–97
guidance of others, using magical
 flight, 242
guided imagery, 16
guidelines, 22. *See also*
 Huna Kupua principles
Gurdjieff, G. I., 223

H
hallucinations, and magical flight,
 218–19, 235
halos. *See* auras
happy bus example, 120–22
harmony, 23, 24, 25
 self-harmony, 291–93
 *there's always another way to do
 anything* story, 34–35
Hawaiian language, 46, 49–50
Hawaiian Mythology
 (Beckwith), 236
Hawaiian proverbs, 292
*Hawaiian Proverbs and Poetical
 Sayings* (Kawena), 24
healing, 12, 14, 15, 16. *See also*
 medical diagnosis
 and emotional energy,
 160, 167
 holistic worldview, 19, 313–15
 legacy of language, 48
 and magical flight, 242, 244
 self, 43, 244
 symbolic worldview, 190, 209,
 212, 213
 thoughtform projection, 148
Healing for the Millions (King),
 116, 314
Healing Relationships (King),
 41, 293
heat-waves, 133, 142, 240
Heinlein, Robert A., 295
helping others, using magical
 flight, 241–43
historical perspectives, auras,
 128–29

holistic worldviews, 6, 16–19
    changing reality, 275–316
    matter, nature of, 263
Holt, Henry, 151
hopelessness, 48
horseshoe game, 168–69
how high can you go principle,
    25, 28. *See also* limitations
human grokking, 313–15. *See also*
    healing
Huna Kupua principles, 21–23
    fifth principle, 191
    as proverbs, 23–25
    seventh principle, 14, 25
    as stories, 26–35
Huna Kupua tradition, 3, 4–6
hunatics, 4
Hunaworks publishing
    company, 103
hunches, 59. *See also* ESP
Hunt, E. K., 130
hurricanes, 258–59, 309–10.
    See also weather
hydration
    and brain physiology, 44
    and physical energy, 51
hypnosis, 16

I
I am what I am and that's all that
    I am, 17
I Ching, 84, 235
I feel, therefore I am, 17
I sense, therefore I am, 17
I think, therefore I am, 17
ideatic telepathy, 74

identifications, hopelessness, 48
identity, holistic worldview, 17–19
Ike, 22
ike papaha. See holistic world
ike papakahi. See objective world
ike papakolu. See symbolic world
ike papalua. See subjective world
illness, 11. *See also* healing;
    medical diagnosis
illusion
    telekinesis, 152–53
    thoughtform projection,
    143–44
Illusions (Bach), 252
images, projecting, 145
imagination, and telepathy, 81, 87,
    91, 92, 108
impressions, sensory, 41
in the spirit of aloha story, 31–32
indication, telepathic, 89
Indo-European languages, 48–49
influencing skills, telepathic
    projection, 105–6
information gathering, using
    magical flight, 243–44
Ingerman, Sandra, 197
inner child, soul retrieval, 196
inner patterns, 300–302
inner world and the outer world
    are without limit, 23, 24,
    25, 28
intellectual static, 94
intellectual telepathy, 71–74
intellectual understanding, 5
intentional beaming, 111–13
intentional broadcasting, 108–9

interdependence.
  See connectedness; unity
interference, telepathic, 93
interior symbols, 184–86
interpretation
  dreams, 176–78
  telepathy, 77–78, 81, 82, 94
intuitions, 59. *See also* ESP
isolation method of magical flight,
  235–36

J
journey, shamanic, 187
joy, 25. *See also* love
jumping jack levitation effect,
  158–59
Jurassic Park (film), 144

K
Kahili, William Wana, 22, 188
Kala, 22
Kalalau Lookout, 119
Kawena, Mary, 24
keep your eyes on the goal story,
  29–30
Kilner, Walter J., 130
  Dangerous Journeys, 23, 196,
    208–15, 248–49
  Earth Energies, 69, 86, 89
  Healing for the Millions,
    116, 314
  Healing Relationships, 41, 293
  Mastering Your Hidden Self,
    176, 188
  poetry, 2, 38, 56, 172, 276, 316

*Urban Shaman and Earth
  Energies*, 84, 176, 184,
  185, 188
Kirlian photography, 131.
  See also auras
knowledge, power of, 39, 40.
  See also learning
  brain physiology, 44–45
  first level change, 42–43
  language, 45–50
  myth of matter, 41
  reality, changing, 52–54
  SE factor, 50–52, 54
  sources of, 4–5, 24–25
Kulagina, Nina, 162–63
kupua. *See Huna Kupua*

L
landslides, 306
language. *See also* communication
  interpretation of dreams,
    177–78
  legacy of, 45–50
  learning, 40. *See also* knowledge
  barriers to, 5
  and brain physiology, 44–45
  reality-changing techniques,
    52–53
  resistance to, 42–43
Lee, Bruce, 102, 157
legends, 26
levels, shifting, 7, 19–20
levitation effect, 152, 154–59.
  See also telekinesis
L-fields, 130

life force. *See* energy
life is in big things, life is in little
    things, 24
Life One, 247
Life Prime, 247, 272–73, 278
lifting things, using telepathic
    projection, 122–23
light
    grokking, 308
    symbol, 203, 205, 206
lightbulb method of seeing
    auras, 140
Lilly, John C., 223
limitations, moving beyond, 23,
    24, 25, 28, 113
living light auras, 135
lobotomy, 91–92
loss of soul, 192, 197–208. *See also*
    soul retrieval
love, 23, 24, 25
    poem, 56
    in the spirit of aloha story,
    31–32
lucid dreaming, 231–32

M
Magic of Believing, The (Bristol),
    164–65
magic mirror, 85
magical flight, 217–19. *See also*
    telepathic projection
    experiencing, 222–31
    methods, 231–39
    occult perspectives, 219–20
    perceptions, other's, 239–40

purpose/uses, 241–45
scientific perspectives, 220–21
shamanic perspective, 221–22
troubleshooting, 246–49
magicians, 152
Makia, 22
making friends, holistic
    worldview, 280–81, 292–93
malleability of matter, 263–72
Mana, 22, 24
Manawa, 22, 24
Marceau, Marcel, 143
Mastering Your Hidden Self (King),
    176, 188
mathematical proportions, 299
matter
    influencing, 263–72
    myth of, 41
M'Bala, 4
measurement, telepathic, 88
measures of truth, 14, 23, 24
medical diagnosis, 208–9
    use of auras, 130, 142–43
    use of pendulum, 90
meditation
    and magical flight, 226–27
    nalu, 285–86
    picture, 233
    purple feather, 251, 253
    techniques for seeing auras,
    141–42
memories, and dreams,
    174–75, 186
memory method of magical
    flight, 233

mental disorders, 218–19, 273
mental strength, 52, 54
merging with the world.
　See grokking
metal, bending, 152, 159–61
metaphors
　computer programming, 256
　third eye, 90–93
meteorites, 273–74
Method Acting, 296
mime, 143–44, 147
mind, as aspect of self,
　291–92, 293
mind control myth of telepathic
　projection, 104–5
mind power, 153–54. *See also*
　telekinesis
mindsets
　model, 8–9
　shifting, 7, 19–20
mirror method of seeing
　auras, 140
misinterpretation, telepathy, 94
missing briefcase example,
　260–61
mob fever, 71
Monroe, Robert, 223
moonlight symbol, 205
motivation, 45
　and dreams, 191
　and telepathy, 106
movie screen technique,
　telepathy, 83
moving between worldviews/
　mindsets, 7, 19–20
moving objects. *See* objects

Mozart, 297–98
music
　language of, 177, 178
　patterns, 297–98
　ukulele, 245, 298, 299, 300
myth of matter, 41
myths/mythology, 26, 129

N
nalu meditation, 285–86
natural patterns, 298–300
nature/natural world
　conversing with, 4, 12–13
　interdependence, 12. *See also*
　　connectedness; unity
neurolinguistics, 16
neutralizing techniques, telepathy,
　71, 101–2
new growth, soul retrieval,
　196–97
New Larousse Encyclopedia
　of Mythology
　(Guirand, ed.), 129
night dreams, 185–86. *See also*
　dreams
nimbus auras, 132–33
nirvana, 230
Nixon, Richard, 71
noninterpretation of telepathy, 94
nothing is impossible principle,
　25, 28

O
objective worldview, 5, 7, 9–12,
　17, 278
　knowledge, power of, 42–43

matter, nature of, 263
myth of matter, 41
reality, changing, 35–54
relationships, 279, 280
soul retrieval, 193
telekinesis, 152
telepathic projection, 120
unexplainable events, 269
objects
communication with, 119–23
levitation effect, 152, 154–59
telekinesis, 123, 161–69
observations. *See Huna Kupua*
principles
occult perspectives of magical
flight, 219–20
ocean waves, 49, 298
olfactory telepathy, 73–74
omens, 4–5, 15
One-Inch Belief, 102
One-Inch Punch, 102, 157
oneness, 17. *See also*
connectedness; unity
OOBE (out-of-body experience).
See magical flight
opening things by
telepathic projection,
122–23
openness, 14
optical illusions, auras as, 138
orange color transmission, 145
ordinary world. *See* objective
worldview
otherness, 17–18
out-of-body experience.
See magical flight

P
pain, 48–49
pain-relief, 43
parallel lives, 227–28, 272–74
and magical flight, 238,
244–45
partiality, telepathic, 96, 99,
100, 101
partner method of magical
flight, 234
passive programming, 257–59
passive telepathy, 69–74
past lives, 14, 172
patterns, 16
grokking, 297–301
symbols, 181–82
Pegasus coincidence, 254
pendulums, use in telepathy,
86–89
perceptions
magical flight, 239–40
myth of matter, 41
time dilation/contraction, 265
perceptual levels. *See* shamanic
worldviews
personal programming.
See programming
personal responsibility, 291
personal sovereignty, 289–91
persuasion skills, and telepathic
projection, 105–6
physical energy, 51, 54
physical exercise, 51
physical strength, 51, 54
physical symbols, techniques for
changing, 181–82

physiology, brain, 44–45, 54
picture meditation, 233
pidgin languages, 46
pineal gland, 91
pink color transmission, 145, 146
placebos, 16
plant example of telepathy, 81–82
plant grokking, 310–12
plant teacher-beings, 206
poetry, 15
    of Serge Kahili King, 2, 38, 56,
        172, 276, 316
    legacy of language, 46–47
poltergeist effects, 152, 159, 161.
    See also telekinesis
Pono, 22
Popeye, 17
positive suggestions, 241–42
posture, 52, 54
power, 23, 24, 25
    of dreams, 187, 190
    of emotion. *See* emotional
        energy
    of knowledge. *See* knowledge
    the secret of fire story, 33–34
    self-empowerment, 289–91
    spots, 142
presence, 23, 24, 25
    where are you? story, 30–31
principles. *See Huna Kupua*
    principles
programming
    influencing experience
        through thought, 256–63
    unity in diversity, 280–93
progressive stretching, 284–85

projection, telepathic.
    See telepathic projection
proportions, mathematical, 299
proverbs, 23–25, 292
psychokinesis, 151–53. *See also*
    telekinesis
psychosis, 218–19, 273
psychotronic devices, 86
public speaking, 146
purple feather coincidence,
    251–54

R
radionics devices, 86
rainbow auras, 134–35
rain-making, 118, 172, 304–5.
    See also weather
reality
    changing. *See* changing reality
    creating, 6–7
    and dreams, 174–75
    as experience, 7–8
receiving telepathy, 70–82
    receiving structures, 82–90
    trouble shooting, 93–98
red color transmission, 145
relationships, holistic worldview,
    279–81, 292–93
relaxation, muscle, 43, 51
    holistic worldview, 284–85
    telekinesis, 166
    telepathy, 77, 102
rematerialization, toothpaste cap,
    262–63
remote dowsing, 89–90
remote influencing. *See* telekinesis

repetitive route method of
    magical flight, 233–34
resistance to learning, 42–43
resonating, 80–82
responsibility, personal, 291
Rhine, J. B., 151
riddles, 34
rituals, 59, 187
    soul retrieval, 198–99, 201–3
    thoughtform symbols, 183

S
samadhi, 230
scanning telepathy, 75–76
scientific perspectives
    auras, 129–31
    magical flight, 220–21
    telekinesis, 152–53
searchlight image, 145
second level experience. *See*
    subjective worldview
secret of fire story, 33–34
self-appreciation, 287–88
self-awareness, 281–84
self development, 244–45
self-empowerment, 289–91
self-esteem, 50–52, 54, 186
self-focus, 285–86
self-harmony, 291–93
self-healing, 43, 244
self-levitation, 154
self-presence, 286–87
self-reconnection, 292
self-relaxation, 284–85
senility, 44
sensations, ESP, 58

sensitivity, 207
sensory impressions, 41
separateness. *See also*
    connectedness; unity
    assumptions of, 10
    sense of, 18
seven elements, 304
seventh *Huna Kupua* principle,
    14, 25
shadow method of seeing
    auras, 141
shamanic dreaming, 187–88
shamanic experience, 6–8
shamanic journey, 187
shamanic worldviews, 1, 5.
    See also holistic; objective;
    subjective; symbolic
    worldview
    magical flight, 221–22
    moving between, 7, 19–20
shapeshifting, 296
shifting mindsets, 7, 19–20
shifts in awareness, 4, 39. *See also*
    experience
sixth sense, 61–62. *See also* ESP
Skin and Bones technique,
    283–84
soul carriers, 194
soul retrieval, 188, 192–215, 296
soul sucker, 194
sovereignty, personal, 289–91
spinning method of magical
    flight, 236–37
spirit, as aspect of self, 291–92, 293
spontaneous attention, 240
spoon-benders, 152, 159–61

sporting events, telekinesis,
167–68
stage magic, 152
Stanislavski, Konstantin, 296
static telepathy, 94–95
stone carving example, 40
stone grokking, 306–7
stories
Huna Kupua principles as,
26–35
magical flight, 236, 248–49
reality, changing, 264–72
unity in diversity, 277–78
storms, 309–10. See also weather
Stranger in a Strange Land
(Heinlein), 295
Strasberg, Lee, 296
streamers (auras), 133–34
strength, mental, 52, 54
strength, physical, 51, 54
stretching, and relaxation, 284–85
subjective worldview, 6, 12–14,
17, 278
changing reality, 55–169
and dreams, 191
illusion, 144
matter, nature of, 263
plant grokking, 311
relationships, 279, 280
telekinesis, 152
telepathic projection, 112,
119, 122
time dilation/contraction, 265
suggestions, positive, 241–42
symbol method of magical
flight, 235

symbolic distortion, telepathy,
95–96, 99, 101
symbolic reception, telepathy, 94,
99, 100, 101
symbolic worldview, 6, 14–16,
17, 172, 278. See also
dreams
changing reality, 171–274
matter, nature of, 263
plant grokking, 311
relationships, 280
symbols
dream, 175, 179–88
language of, 178
synchronicity, time, 13

T
t-field thoughtform projection,
143–48
talismans, 16
tarot cards, 84
telekinesis, 151–53
bending metal, 152, 159–61
levitation effect, 152–53,
154–59
mind power, 153–54
moving objects, 161–69
telepathic projection, 103–4.
See also magical flight
beaming, 109–13
broadcasting, 106–9
consciousness, 222
mind control myth, 104–5
non-human subjects, 113–23
persuasive/influencing skills,
105–6

Telepathic Receiving Device
  (TRD), 86
telepathy, 13, 64–65. *See also* ESP;
  subjective worldview
  benefits of, 65–66
  energy, 67–69
  experiments, 99–101
  and magical flight, 222
  neutralizing techniques, 71,
    101–2
  receiving structures, 82–90
  shifting mindsets, 20
  third eye, 90–93
  trouble shooting, 93–98
  types, 69–82
teleportation, 266–68
Texas conundrum, 261–62
t-field thoughtform projection,
  143–48
*there's always another way to do
  anything* story, 34–35
third eye metaphor, 90–93
third level experience.
  See symbolic world
this reminds me of myself
  game, 53
thought is the chief, activity is
  the follower, 24
thoughtform projection, 143–48,
  238–39, 305
thoughtform symbols, 183–84
thoughts, and experience. *See*
  experience, influencing
Three Musketeers, The (Dumas), 47
three selves, 291–92
time dilation/contraction, 264–66

time synchronicity, 13
toothpaste cap rematerialization,
  262–63
tornadoes, 309–10. *See also* weather
trance states, 4
translucent forms, 240
trauma
  and brain physiology, 44
  loss of soul, 192
  soul retrieval, 197–208
TRD (Telepathic Receiving
  Device), 86
tribal identity, 18
troubleshooting
  magical flight, 246–49
  telepathy, 93–98
trust, 58, 185
truth is measured by results,
  14, 23, 24
tsunamis, grokking, 304–5
tuning in to a dream, 184–85
tuning, telepathy, 76–80, 84
types of magical flight, 224–31

U
UFOs, 268
ukulele music, 245, 298, 299, 300
unexplainable events, 266–72
unicorns, 83
unintentional beaming, 109–10
unintentional broadcasting, 106–7
union with Christ, 230
unity, 17, 277–79. *See also*
  connectedness; grokking
  personal programming, 280–93
  and relationships, 279–80

unstructured interior symbols,
184–86
Urban Shaman and Earth Energies
(King), 84, 176, 184,
185, 188

V

validity, telepathy, 81, 82, 90
values, personal, 10–12
verb *to be*, 47–48
verbal language, 177. *See also*
language
verbal telepathy, 72–73
videophone technique, 83
visions, 60. *See also* ESP
visual telepathy, 72
visualization
telepathic projection, 109
therapies, 16, 20
vitamin deficiencies, 45
volcanoes, 306–7
voodoo, 104
vril drops, 69

W

walking exercise, 51
wall image, 257
Wana Kahili, 4, 6
warrior shamanic tradition, 193

wasps, communication with,
115–16
water bottle example, 282
water grokking, 304–5
waves, 49, 53, 263, 276, 298
weather
communication with, 117–19
grokking, 309–10
hurricanes, 258–59, 309–10
rain-making, 118, 172, 304–5
websites, 152–53
Welcome Home (Ingerman), 197
werewolves, 296
what if? game, 53–54
what you see is what you get story,
26–27
where are you? story, 30–31
white color transmission, 145, 147
wind grokking, 309–10. *See also*
weather
wine taster example, 62
world is what you think it is, the,
6, 23
world of being. *See* holistic
worldview
World of Warcraft role-playing
game, 196
worldviews, shamanic.
See shamanic worldviews

About the Author

Serge Kahili King, PhD, is a husband, father, friend, shaman, author, teacher, storyteller, psychologist, and computer gamer, in that order. He also loves Hawaiian culture, learning new things, and collecting rocks.

He has studied intensively with Hawaiian, African, and Mongolian shamans; has traveled to more than fifty countries (so far); and is the executive director of Aloha International, a worldwide network of people helping to make the world a better place.

Currently, Dr. King lives next to an active volcano on the island of Hawaii with his wife and four computers and occupies himself with writing books, teaching classes, developing a virtual Huna Center in Second Life, and helping to preserve the native forest.

For more information, please visit the following websites:
www.huna.org
www.huna.net
www.alohainternational.org
www.sergeking.com